The
FINDHORN
book of

Everyday
Abundance

by
Karen Hood-Caddy

© Karen Hood-Caddy 2004

First published by Findhorn Press 2004

ISBN 1 84409 031 0

British Library Cataloguing-in-Publication Data.
A catalogue record for this book is available from
the British Library.

Edited by Shari Mueller
Cover by Thierry Bogliolo
Internal design by Karin Bogliolo
Cover background photograph by Digital Vision
Cover central photograph ©PhotoDisc

Printed and bound by WS Bookwell, Finland

Published by
Findhorn Press
305a The Park, Findhorn
Forres IV36 3TE
Scotland, UK
tel 01309 690582
fax 01309 690036
e-mail: info@findhornpress.com

www.findhornpress.com

TABLE OF CONTENTS

TO MY SON, JASON,

FOR SHARING HIS ABUNDANT HEART

AND TO ROD,

FOR SHARING HIS ABUNDANT LIFE

MY DEEPEST GRATITUDE FOR

FINDHORN AND TO FINDHORN PRESS

AND TO THE MANY PEOPLE WHO

SHARED THEIR ABUNDANT JOURNEYS.

Karen Hood-Caddy

INTRODUCTION

THE GARDEN OF ABUNDANCE

"Who looks outside, dreams. Who looks inside, awakens."
—Carl Jung

Abundant people are easy to recognize. Generosity emanates from them. You can almost feel the plenitude of possibilities erupting from their centers like seeds in big-faced sunflowers. If abundant people had a sound, it would be the thrum of some lush operatic aria that makes your crystal glasses sing.

Findhorn was born from the seed of abundance. When Peter and Eileen Caddy, along with Dorothy Maclean, nestled their small caravan into the sand dunes near Findhorn village over 40 years ago, they had no financial resources. Peter had just been let go as manager of the hotel at Cluny Hill and there was barely enough money to feed themselves and the three Caddy boys. Peter, however, had learned through his various spiritual training never to give attention to the problem, but to focus only on the solution. So what did he do? He started a garden.

The garden was the beginning place. Peter's garden offered many lessons but there was one quintessential teaching: that abundance is the natural state of the universe. Nature demonstrates this at every turn. All you have to do is cut open a tomato and you will see not just one or two seeds, but dozens of seeds tucked into the juicy caverns.

Since the garden was the beginning place for the Caddys, I shall use it as an ongoing metaphor throughout the book. The material itself is divided into four parts. Part One explains how to prepare your inner soil, Part Two shows how to choose and grow what I call your "soul seeds," Part Three describes a variety of tools for doing the work and Part Four completes the book by talking about how you can move beyond creating abundance to becoming abundance itself.

MY INTRODUCTION TO ABUNDANCE

My introduction to the concept of abundance happened when I first went to Findhorn in the late 1970s. As part of the Experience Week, a workshop in which all newcomers to the community participate, we read David Spangler's book, *The Laws of Manifestation*. It affected me deeply. At that stage in my life, I was just getting a toehold on the colossal idea that I could be a Conscious Creator and this book was like finding a map to the treasure. I decided to try out the principles and set my sites on 'manifesting' a pair of red shoes. As the book suggested, I formed a clear picture of the shoes in my mind, then held that picture in my awareness. As Spangler recommended, I didn't worry about 'how' the shoes were going to come my way, but trusted in the inherent abundance of the universe to bring them to me – which the universe did, and promptly, too, I might add.

When the imagined red shoes arrived into my life so easily, I was elated. Up until this point, I had thought of myself as a mere recipient of whatever Life decided to put my way. To me, Life had been like a fickle friend, sometimes being good to me, sometimes not, but regardless of which side of the teeter-totter I was temporarily on, there didn't seem to be much I could do to affect what I got. The idea that I could enter into the game of creating my life was utterly fascinating. I continued with my experiments.

During my 7 years at Findhorn and the many years since, I have been honing my creating abundance skills. At the beginning, I focussed mostly on creating physical things (like red shoes), but as my manifestation muscles became stronger, I tried my hand at creating nonphysical things like love and forgiveness. I found that the laws of manifestation worked regardless of the realm to which I applied them.

As a result, I've been able to bring to flower all of my heart's most cherished desires. (Interestingly enough, the last of these was created through my involvement with this book.) Although I know there are still some areas of my life I'd like to create differently, I feel continually grateful for the garden of living I have created. My wish in this book is to offer these tools and insights so you can create your own life garden and grow your own dreams to full blossom.

NEW 'ABUNDANCE' RESEARCH

Recently there have been some new developments in understanding not only how the process of abundance works, but ways in which the process can be accelerated. These new tools and technologies are able to recalibrate our energetic systems so we can be in a more complete alignment with what we wish to create.

In the early days of 'abundance' thinking, there was a fair bit of philosophy, but few tools to actually work the philosophy. The only tool I can remember using, other than visualization, was the practice of writing affirmations. Books on abundance advised people to write pages of affirmative statements, sometimes even saying them out loud or saying them while holding a mirror. Unfortunately, for many of us, saying affirmations felt like trying to stick globs of gelatin to a concrete wall. They simply didn't work and all the repetition in the world was not going to get them to work.

Research in Applied Kinesiology may offer an explanation. In experiments where participants made statements they didn't think were true, their muscles tested weak. When they made statements they did think were true, their muscles held firm and tested strong. For me, this means that however pleasant affirmations may be to say, they aren't powerful enough to override the beliefs and energetic patterns that are already installed in our systems.

As well as using affirmations, the earlier books on abundance advised us to watch our thoughts and make them more congruent with what we wanted to create. At this stage in my acquisition of abundance skills, I put Henry Ford's maxim on my wall: "If you think you can, you can. If you think you can't, you can't."

Despite the fact that I learned to be a fastidious custodian of my thought processes, I found that developing cognitive awareness of my thoughts was not enough. Yes, it helped to see my thought patterns, but it was like being aware of the weeds in a garden – my cognitive awareness didn't get rid of the weeds and until I did that, too much of my energy was being devoured by the weeds for any new seeds to grow. I planted new seeds anyway and did have some success growing my heart's desires, but they grew like any seeds in a weed-infested garden – they struggled and grew slowly. I knew I needed more than cognitive awareness if I was going to completely change my life into the abundant one I wanted. What I needed was something bigger, more comprehensive and perhaps more pervasive – I needed a technology to completely pull out the old limiting beliefs that had rooted themselves in my energetic system. Only then would I have the space and energy to plant and grow new seeds for my life.

Then Energy Medicine came along.

ENERGY MEDICINE

Energy Medicine is any modality that deliberately realigns the energy field into a healthier, more congruent pattern. Energy Medicine does this by impacting a variety of different systems (chakras*, meridians, the aura, to name a few) in and around the body and recalibrating them into perfect alignment. What's exciting about these techniques, is that not only are they easy to learn, but they can also be self-administered. This permits people to self-regulate their own energy field and to do so with precision. They will also allow people to work with themselves on a micro level, altering smaller nuances of energy so their congruence is more total and complete.

What this means for me is that I no longer have to wait until I am off track to initiate an interrupt. In the past, I would only work on myself when

---

*see page 126

my life wasn't going well or when I was in so much pain that I was forced to take action. Now, I can regulate myself on a moment-to-moment basis, recalibrating my system all the time so it's vibrating at the level I want. For the first time in my life, I feel like I can consciously create who I am.

In my experience, adding the energy medicine techniques to the tools of cognitive awareness creates a unique opportunity for people to become true masters of themselves. These paired skills will permit people to create what they want from inside out, and therefore free them from having to manipulate the outside world in order to get their needs met.

For example, in order for most people to feel joy or love, there has to be an outside stimulus, some event or purchase, perhaps. We imagine that our well-being is determined by what happens outside of us and therefore, most of us put a great amount of energy into managing that 'out there.' But with these new techniques, people will be able to create the feelings of joy and love through conscious choice.

Does that mean you will be able to create whatever you like? I remember when I first started reading about the process of manifesting and attracting, it used to upset me if books made such promises. What hubris I thought. Even a Manifesting Magnet can't create youth. Or endless life. Or take away a family member's paranoid schizophrenia.

Not yet, perhaps, but if we could time-travel back even one hundred years, before planes and cars and computers, the inhabitants of that earlier world would have a difficult time believing all the creations we've made. At the very least, they'd be utterly astounded. As they should be. What we currently are able to create IS astounding.

Although we haven't yet been able to create perpetual youth or cure schizophrenia, one day we will. It's just that some 'manifestations' are going to take longer than others. Some might take more time than our individual lifetimes permit. Nevertheless, we are creators in training. We are on our way to becoming Gods in our own right.

CLAIMING OUR POWER

Even if a particular situation requires longer than my life span to create, that doesn't mean any of us are powerless. At any given time, each of us is totally in charge of creating how we respond to a given situation. Buddhists have been teaching this truth for years, encouraging seekers to search out the space between what happens to us and how we respond to what happens to us. Whenever I am able to do this, to wiggle into the space between what happens and my response to what happens, I always feel as if I've found a hole in the garden wall. New territory opens up in front of my eyes.

Finding that gap between what happens and how we respond to what happens is important because it's that very place where we experience the power of our consciousness to change things. Let's imagine, for example, that I want a new job. I want a new job because I believe that new job will make me happy. If a new job doesn't appear, as it might not right away, I might just decide to let go of thinking that my happiness is contingent on getting a new job. I may just decide to be happy anyway. Meanwhile, I might keep looking for a job, but it will be from a different energy, a more expanded energy. My guess is that I will be more likely to find a new job because of this expanded energy. After all, there are thousands of new jobs out there, and the more expanded my energy field, the more likely I am to hear about the perfect one for me.

This book is going to give you lots of tools for creating that job, or creating whatever it is that you want to create. But it is going to go beyond that. It is going to teach you the skills to put yourself in an energetic field where the jobs (or whatever it is you want to create) will begin to come to you. Then, it's going to go even further. It's going to help you become abundance itself. Because for me, true abundance is a spiritual state that involves the very essence of Who We Are.

Sometimes in its quest for the Light, the New Age has inadvertently promoted the idea that you can just have the good stuff. We can certainly have more good stuff and I'm going to outline lots of methods in this book for doing exactly that, but spiritual abundance is more than attracting the good . When someone is in a state of spiritual abundance, there is complete alignment between the body, mind and soul. An elegant flow begins to move through their lives. People in this state vibrate at such an attuned level, they naturally attract what's right for them. And when something difficult presents itself, there is no resistance to it, nor is there any judgment. Truly abundant people know their inner state is what determines the rest of their lives and they take charge of that inner state. They also deeply trust that whatever comes towards them is something that they have drawn into their lives for some reason.

That's why truly abundant people have an air of ease about them. They've moved past any desperation to always be pulling in the good stuff, or attracting what shines. They know that what shines comes from their own hearts.

When you know that all the Light you need comes from within, a new comfortability with the dark comes too. As a result, Life can be greeted on its own terms. This deep acceptance of the Way Things Are leads to a delicious state of grace.

So the art of abundance is really a sort of spiritual alchemy. It allows you to convert whatever comes (or gets thrown) your way into gold. Or, do what Peter Caddy, the gardener, did and turn it into rich and rejuvenating compost. And speaking of compost, get your garden tools – it's time to begin.

PART ONE

PREPARING YOUR INNER SOIL

Chapter 1

SETTING YOUR INTENTION: CLEARING THE LAND

"Twenty years from now you will be more disappointed by the things
that you didn't do than by the ones you did do.
So throw off the bowlines.
Sale away from the safe harbor. Explore. Dream. Discover."
—Mark Twain

Are you aware that you're making a choice right now? You are choosing to read this book. You might make another choice in a moment, but right now, you are reading these words on this page. As you read, I hope you will choose to get excited and get your life moving, but you may not. Whether you do or not will largely depend on your intention.

To me, intention is like a spade. It is the first tool you will need to clear the land so you can begin creating your garden.

Intention is conscious choice. Each and every one of us makes hundreds of choices every day, but how many do we make consciously? Too often, we make choices by default – by taking no action, we let the momentum of what we've already set up in our lives take over. When we do this, we let Life happen to us. But when we make an intention, we begin to happen to Life.

If you want to know the choices you've been making, simply review your life. The state of your body is the tabulation of your food choices, the state of your relationship world is the tabulation of your emotional choices.

Sometimes there is great resistance to this idea that we create our lives. Like frustrated gardeners standing on fields of sand or clay, we complain about the soil conditions or rant about the bugs or the weather. However, when we understand abundance more fully and how to create it with the spade of intention, we begin to understand that it doesn't matter what the soil conditions are. Peter Caddy will attest to that – with Dorothy's and Eileen's guidance, he grew thirty-pound cabbages in sand!

So, let's begin by looking at the garden you've created so far. Is it the garden you want? Are there some areas that need an overhaul? Some new plants you'd like to grow?

When I'm not writing books, I work as a Life Coach so I'm used to asking people, "What are you creating?" Even over the phone, I can feel people squirm at the self-responsibility this question implies. For the most part, people aren't used to taking full responsibility for their lives. It's easier to imagine that my life has simply 'happened' to me. When I view it that way, I let myself off the hook.

ＴＡＫＩＮＧ ＲＥＳＰＯＮＳＥ-ＡＢＩＬＩＴＹ ＦＯＲ ＷＨＡＴ ＷＥ ＣＲＥＡＴＥ

As a coach, I know that the moment a client takes response-ability for what they've created, the work can begin. One of the factors I've noticed that increases a person's ability to take response-ability is a willingness to set blame and judgment aside. This is so pronounced that it is now one of the indicators I look for at the beginning of the coaching relationship. If I encounter someone who is highly self-blaming and judgmental, I know their growth is going to be slowed down considerably. Blame and judgment are like huge rocks in the middle of your garden. You don't want them. Roll them aside.

So, without any self-judgment or blame, make an assessment of your life so far. To help you along, draw 3 plant pots. Label them 'Love' and 'Joy' and 'Fulfillment.' Without thinking too much about it, let your hand draw something in each pot. Don't worry if it doesn't look artistic, that's not what this is about. And don't think about it, just find a paper and pen and do it.

I'm going to proceed to talk about this exercise now, but do note if you've made the choice not to find a pen and paper and do it. Is this a choice that serves your growth? Without beating yourself up, ask yourself what would have to change right now for you to make a different choice, then do it.

Now, suspend your wish to assess and judge what you've drawn, just look at your drawings. Are there fully grown, lush plants in each pot? Is one or more of the pots full of some spindly plant or no plant at all? Perhaps something altogether different showed up in one of the pots. Whatever happened, do not judge. Not judging doesn't mean you can't have feelings. You might feel sad about the fact that your 'joy' plant is so small or that your 'love' plant has no flowers. Note the feelings, note their strength, but leave all judgment and self-recrimination out of it.

What you see in these pots is a result of the thousands of choices you've made so far in your life. Would you like something different, or more pleasing to grow in these pots? If you don't make a different choice, and fire up that choice with intention, you will create more of what you've already created. Intention is choice with power. If it were a vehicle it would be a souped-up muscle car. It will get you where you are going fast.

WHAT INTENTION ISN'T

Sometimes people get 'intention' and 'will' mixed-up. People who don't understand the difference may find themselves struggling unnecessarily. Intention is not will or will power and has more to do with clarity than push. In terms of the energy centers in the body, it involves the third chakra because it relates to personal power and identity. When we choose something from the third chakra, it is because we know it is deeply right for us. It is Who We Are.

I remember a client of mine, Nancy, telling me how she got herself to leave an abusive relationship. "I finally got that's it's just not who I am to be treated like that," she said. It didn't fit her at the deepest level of her sense of Self. When she got in touch with that, she didn't have to struggle to get out of this relationship or work at it, she simply set it aside like a garment that no longer fit.

Intention is different from will, and different from wishing, too.

To demonstrate this, let's do another exercise. The motivational guru, Tony Robbins, from whom I have learned a lot, offers this exercise in one of his programs. First of all, think of something you'd like to create. Now spend a moment and wish for it. As you do, notice how you feel. Then, change the verb so that instead of *wishing* for this event or item, *expect* it. Notice any difference?

When I did this exercise, I wished for a movie contract for one of my novels. I've been wishing for this for a few years so wishing for it again felt familiar. It also made me feel like a kid with her nose pressed up against the bakery window, wishing for something that was being withheld from me. Since I'd wished for this before with no success, the act of wishing for it again seemed to deepen the widening rut of disappointment and fill it with more feelings of powerlessness.

When I changed the verb and imagined *expecting* the film contract, there was an immediate rush of feeling in my body. A sense of possibility zoomed towards me. I felt more hopeful that my dream might come true, but the fulfillment of the dream still didn't feel as if it had anything to do with me – I still felt like a powerless recipient of Life's happenstance.

Now I'm going to add my own twist to this exercise and take it one step further. Let's change the verb from *expect*, to *intend* and apply it to what you want to create. Notice the difference. When I did this with the film contract, I felt a strong, energetic shift. More of me had suddenly become involved. I was no longer a recipient, but an active creator. I felt the same sense of excitement I felt when my father first put the car keys in my hand.

INTENᗞING FROM WᕼO YOU ARE

For intention to reach its full power, it needs to be aligned with the truth of your spiritual essence. When intention is fired from your soul, you won't have to work so hard to make it happen.

But what if you're not sure who you are? You may say, "I know I'm an accountant or I'm a wife, or I'm a dancer, but other than that, I'm not sure. How would I know that?"

First of all, let me say this: it's not unusual to be unsure of Who You Are. Our culture is so busy telling us who we ought to be, what we're supposed to look like and think like, that it's not easy to access our inner knowing. But that doesn't mean this knowing isn't available.

Close your eyes and think about a time that you felt supremely joyful and in love with Life. What were you doing? Who were you with? What was the environment like around you? Now reconnect with another memory when you felt joyful. And one more. Now look for similarities in these events. For me, each situation involved 3 things: being outside in nature, feeling intimately connected either with myself or with intimate friends and lastly, being involved in some physical activity like hiking or paddling my kayak. What are the similarities in your peak memory moments?

Now, choose the juiciest experience. Allow all the lovely feelings of that joy and in-love-with-life feeling to reverberate through your body. See if you can turn up the dial to make the feeling even more vivid. Remember the colors as vividly as you can, the aromas, the textures and sounds.

That heightened sense of life is Who You Are. Memorize this feeling and use it as a sort of vibrational template. Think of some of your usual life activities and hold them up to this template – is there an energetic resonance or dissonance? Discard any judgment. Just assess.

If you want, you can make an intention to begin aligning your entire life with this vibrational template. If you choose to do this, make the intention from your heart, not from your head. And do it now. Now is the only moment you have.

A friend of mine, Cinder Hammond, told me about an experience she had with intention when she was attending Jean Houston's Mystery School. Every year, as part of the Mystery School curriculum, Jean conducts a special Gifting Ceremony. Participants spend time before the ceremony deeply attuning to themselves and choosing their most important heart's desire.

"It's a wonderful exercise," Cinder says. "It really makes you get clear on what's important to you."

After much thinking, Cinder decided she wanted to choose the creation of a life partner and spoke that request aloud to Jean in an atmosphere of support from all those assembled at the ceremony.

"Speaking it aloud helps you to claim it," says Cinder. "And it also gives life to your intention in that once you've put it out there, the world starts to respond."

That night, Cinder had an important dream. She dreamed that she was going to meet her partner, who was English, during a trip that Jean Houston was leading to England that summer. Cinder had signed up for the trip the previous year, however, as the departure date approached, ill health prevented her from going. Cinder says she temporarily questioned whether she was going to have to forfeit meeting her life partner as well as the trip, but decided that "something else must be in the works." As indeed it was.

"What's so funny about all of this," says Cinder, "is that I did meet my partner during the trip. While Jean and the rest of the tour were in England, I met Martyn in Canada. He is an Englishman living here now!"

Cinder's story is a wonderful example of setting an intention and then releasing the process.

"What I do when I'm making an intention," said Cinder, "is to energize it with as much emotion as I can, then give thanks for it already being true. That's the part I need to focus on, not how it's going to happen. I've learned to leave that up to the angels.

WhO YOU ARE NOT

Part of the reason Cinder was successful in attracting her life partner was that her intention was completely in line with her Soul. She knew having a partner was part of who she was. She also knew the converse: that not having a life partner would be living a lie to her truest self.

Sometimes knowing Who We Are comes from experiencing Who We Are Not. We all have had times when we've acted from places that are not Who We Are. Taking my own life for an example, when I was young, I smoked cigarettes. Like most people, I had a completely love-hate relationship with smoking, but nonetheless, I was thoroughly addicted. I smoked throughout my teens and finally, in my twenties, my body got sick of the way I was treating it and shut down one of my lungs. In the hospital with pneumonia, I wasn't able to smoke and was too sick to want to. Besides that, lying in a hospital bed gave me a lot of time to think and reconnect with myself. I quit smoking, but I also made other changes in my life. I took up yoga and meditation and found myself getting on a whole new track with myself. Even now, I am grateful for that time of inner reflection. It helped me connect deeply with what I was really about.

Sometimes, we make mistakes and have to experience over and over what it's like to live out of alignment with our Souls before we can make a change. Most of us move along our evolutionary path through the process of making mistakes. We all have learned this way and many of us will continue to learn this way, through the school of hard knocks. The method is slow and onerous, but it will get us to evolve eventually. Some of the techniques I'm going to be describing in this book, however, will give us the opportunity to create change more easily and with less effort through what I call spiritual attunement. Spiritual attunement and abundance are basically the same thing. Using these techniques will involve intention.

USING INTENTION AT EVERY MOMENT

Abraham, a channeled entity who speaks through Jerry and Ester Hicks, suggests that we use the power of intention not just for the big things in life, but the small things as well. We can set an intention for how we want a meeting to go, for how efficiently we want to spend the next hour of our time, or for the state we want to be in at the end of the day.

I have found this advice to be immeasurably helpful. I also use the power of intention to create particular emotional states. If you're like me, it probably feels as if various moods just 'arrive,' with the unpredictability of a weather system, but moods can be created, too. Setting an intention is the first step in that process. Try it now. Set an intention for how you want to vibrate in the next hour. You'll notice as you move into this hour, how your intention will steer you towards what you want and away from what you don't want like a deep keel on a sailboat.

Chapter 2

DESERVINGNESS: OPENING UP THE SOIL

"You deserve to attract Divine abundance
because you and God are the same."
—Wayne Dyer

Once you have an intention to create a garden of abundance, you can turn your attention to the state of your inner soil. Imagine trying to sow seeds into an impenetrable landscape of clay. Clay is too hard for seed planting and is not interested in being pierced by anything, let alone the seeds of new possibilities.

To me, feelings of unworthiness are a sure sign of a clay-like emotional body. When we feel undeserving, our energetic system stiffens up and becomes a barrier to penetration, even to the most wondrous of possibilities. To illustrate this, think about the last time you tried to give a compliment to someone with low self-esteem. Could you feel your comment going into the earth of that person and warming his or her heart? Not likely. People who have stocked their inner shelves with denigrating self-concepts have no room for the arrival of an unexpected shipment of something good. And when something good does come their way, they turn it away. Sometimes if you compliment such a person you will notice that person holding their hands up in front of them in a sort of 'stop' gesture.

If we are convinced we don't have value, we will consciously or unconsciously repel comments or actions that are valuing. Our friends learn not to bother trying to deliver valuing comments, which, if our esteem is really low, we will interpret as further confirmation of our lack of worth. Sad as it may be, this is how we inadvertently 'train' our friends and family to treat us in certain ways. If we block the good energy, the less than good will have an open highway to our hearts.

For most of us, despite the fact that our feelings of self-worth fluctuate from time to time, there is a core sense of how much we value ourselves. Would you like to assess your own feelings of worthiness? Here are some statements. Rate yourself from 1 to 10 (10 being high, 1 being low) as to how fully you resonate with the sentiment.

WORTHINESS SELF TEST

- I have friends who value me for who I am, not for anything I do or have accomplished.

- When someone gives me a compliment, I say, "Thank you for noticing," or words to that effect.

- When someone offers to help me, or assist me, I accept the gift of that offering without feeling that I have to pay them back or offer something in return.

- I regularly and repeatedly tell myself how valuable I am.

- I am the first to notice my innate wonderful qualities.

- When something very lush and lovely comes my way, I accept it with relaxation and ease.

- If I make a mistake, I don't beat up my Beingness by saying things like, "I'm so stupid," but use what happened as feedback and make adjustments.

- If someone behaves badly towards me, I am clear that I don't deserve such treatment and state this easily.

- I regularly spend money to augment my deepest well-being, whether that involves taking a holiday, investing in a course or buying the coaching I need to feel empowered.

- I expect people to treat me wonderfully.

Add up your score and see how you did. The total possible points add up to 100, but most of us will score far below that. Don't be surprised. We live in a culture that does not deeply feed people on inner levels, so most of us have some worthiness wounds. For some of us, these wounds originate from early in our childhood when our core sense of value was becoming formed. Although many of us received unconditional love as infants, it wasn't long before our parents, who most probably also suffered from low self-worth, began to put pressure on us to make them proud. To please them, we learned to perform. It's no coincidence that first-born children are the highest achievers.

Whatever the origins of our unworthiness, the wound of it remains to be healed. Many people try to cover up the wound by either accomplishing or acquiring. Both of these strategies can make us feel good for a while, but unworthiness is like quicksand and soon pulls our trophies into its depths, leaving us struggling to repeat the accomplishing and acquiring until we're exhausted as many movie stars and celebrities have experienced.

I can speak to this from personal experience. Before I was published, I used to dream about how wonderful everything would be when I finally saw my name in print. One book came, then another, and now I have 3 novels out and this book you are reading, but I still have to pay attention to feeding my deep sense of inner value.

For most of us, it's a shock to realize there is nothing 'out there' that is going to make everything all right. By and large, healing work is an inside job. It requires alone time and a commitment to doing our own inner work.

Here are some actions I use and often recommend to people for increasing self worth. Try them. If you take your time and do them with heartfelt intention, you will find them powerfully healing.

INCREASING YOUR SELF-VALUE

- As you go about your daily life, focus more on what you are than on what you do. Try tuning into yourself as a *presence*. Be aware of emitting the kind of energy you value. Trust that your biggest contribution to the world is Who You Are, not what you do.

- At the end of every day, review what you feel good about, then go behind those activities and find the innate personality qualities from which those actions sprung. For example, if you gave a birthday card to a friend, you would say, "I am a considerate, thoughtful person." If you wrote an excellent report, you might say, "I am a good thinker." Keep affirming the gifts of your Beingness.

By distilling your actions down to the qualities that birthed them, you will become more aware of your innate gifts. These gifts are part of your essence and were given to you before birth. What are your particular gifts? Are you creative, loving, kind, forgiving, joyful, sweet-souled, generous, funny? These qualities are part of the wonder of Who You Are. Acknowledge and celebrate them.

- When someone says something complimentary, try putting your hand on your sacred heart (below your throat, but above your breast area) and let the comment in. Feed yourself with it. Repeat the comment to yourself several times in the following days. Don't gobble it up and be done with it, but savor it like an emotional cookie. Also, appreciate the person who gave you the compliment. That will ensure you get more.

- Spend time in the arms of your spiritual helpers. A few years ago, I was co-leading a workshop at Findhorn with Nina Menrath, an art therapist from California, when an extraordinary thing happened. We were all working quietly at an art exercise when I felt a colossal wave of energy wash over me. The energy was warm and not threatening in any way, but it was too much like a tidal wave for me not to feel overwhelmed. I stood up and went outside in an attempt to gain control. Nothing like this had ever happened to me before and I didn't know how to handle it. Once I was outside, the energy continued to flood over me. I let go of my resistance to it and as I did, a wonderful feeling of warmth and love flowed over me. It was almost as if some gigantic Cosmic Mother had found me and taken me into her arms. Remembering the experience brings tears to my eyes even now. At the time, it made me feel young and vulnerable. This "energy" seemed to know this and became all the more soothing.

Like a spiritual orphan who'd just found its parents, I cried for days after this event. Somehow I managed to pull myself together during workshop times, but outside of the workshop, I just let myself be held in the arms of this Great Mother.

Over the years, I have spent lots of time with this Cosmic Mother. When I first imagined myself with her, I was small and lay in her arms like an infant. A few months later, I was a toddler on her lap, then a teenager. These days I sit beside her and we hold each other's hands. My heart swells with gratitude even now as I write about her.

The point I am making is that there are all kinds of nourishing Spiritual energies out there – angels, guides, presences. When I lived at Findhorn I became very aware of one such Spiritual energy, the Angel of Findhorn. Since leaving, I haven't been tuning into this Presence much, but recently, because of this book, I have been renewing my relationship to this angel in my meditations and extraordinary things have been happening. Abundance has been flooding towards me like never before and I'm blossoming as if I've been transplanted into an energetic greenhouse. Never before have I felt so supported on both inner and outer levels.

The reason I am talking about angels and other healing presences is because I think it's difficult to heal one's self-worth without help from the spiritual realms. In my experience, only spiritual energy can go to the depth of one's being and that's how deep the healing needs to be if we are going to move fully into a life of abundance. For us to know our intrinsic value, we need to know we are loved just because we live and breathe. To me, that kind of love lives primarily in the spiritual arena.

I have a dear friend, Serene Chazan, who works as a psychotherapist in California. Serene has experienced every kind of therapy and has been a participant in all kinds of workshops on personal growth. However, it was only when she began her spiritual work that her deepest wounds began to heal.

This is what she says about her evolving healing process. "I have found that my truest self-esteem has nothing to do with how I am, or am seen, in worldly matters. It's how I am in my heart, which has to do with an inner sense of completeness that is not related to the world as such. And it's come about through my spiritual work, by experiencing myself as God might experience me. Sometimes I just imagine being held in God's arms and being appreciated and loved for all that I am, for all my juiciness and aliveness and strength and joy. By letting in God's love for me, I can let in my own love for me more completely."

The kind of deep healing that is required for us to know our own value, requires a call to the energies in the spiritual realms. Only energy that large and pervasive can heal the depth of our wounds. But these energies will enter into our lives only by invitation. So give them permission to enter. Even if you're not sure whether such realms or helpers exist, invite them to help you and see what happens. Their help may not come in the timing you had imagined or even in the form you imagined, but knock and the door will open.

A HEALING MEDITATION FOR SELF-WORTH

This meditation will work directly on healing your inner sense of value. To do it, find a quiet place and assume a meditative posture. The chakras need to be in a vertical position, so it's best to be sitting in some fashion, either on a chair or on the floor with your back straight.

Calm yourself and establish a deep, rhythmic breathing pattern. Imagine that you are sitting in a waterfall and that a cascade of lovely luminescent energy is washing over you like water. Give the energy a color, perhaps silver or gold, and imagine that it's warm and nourishing essence is splashing down over you.

Now imagine that you open a gate that's just above your head (your crown chakra) and let this warm, nourishing energy flood down into your body. Feel it flow into your mind in waves of loving thoughts, feel it washing down through your body, allowing love and acceptance to enter every cell in your body and soul.

Let this cascade of loving energy move through you; feel it healing and bringing love to every part of your being. Let the warm, loving water wash away all stress, all feelings of inadequacy and unworthiness. Imagine this healing energy is planting a new seed into each and every cell, a seed that says, "I am truly valuable."

Whisper this to yourself if it feels right and imagine every part of you aligning with this truth. Bask in the energy you've created for as long as you can. And repeat the meditation often.

OṪꞪER SELF-VALUING BEꞪAVIORS

Don't get me wrong, I'm not advocating being stingy with others. What I'm suggesting is that you give so fully to yourself that you have an abundance to share with others. To me, this is the new model of giving, to be like a fountain, continually flowing with energy. The image of a fountain is a good one, for some water always has to be moving back into the pond at the same time as some is shooting out into the air. Because the fountain is perfectly balanced between taking water in and pushing water out, there is no worry about depletion. Depleting yourself to give to someone else is a sure way to block the flow. This is not abundance. Sacrificing is never abundance. Besides, who feels good about receiving something when it's at someone else's expense?

A POWERFUL QUESTION

Because of my work as a coach, I have learned the deepest respect for the power of questions. A good question is like a dynamite stick. It can blast apart the most dense and compacted energy. Here's one of my favorites. Use it before you do any activity for the next few days and it will reveal to you not only how self-valuing you are but will show you where your challenges are.

The question is this:

Does this activity (e.g., eating this food, having this relationship, thinking these thoughts, etc.) make me value myself more or less?

This question can be used as a keel to keep you on your self-valuing track. And when you do get off track – and you will from time to time

– notice what pushes you into self-denigrating thoughts or actions. Then, do the meditation described above or pick one of the tools in the energy medicine section in Chapter Six. Take immediate response-ability for yourself and your energy. Create yourself!

Chapter 3

GRATITUDE:
ENRICHING THE SOIL

"Many people are waiting for prosperity. It cannot come in the future.
Gratitude for the present moment and the fullness of life
now is true prosperity."
—Eckhart Tolle in *The Power of Now*

There is a universal law: what goes around comes around. Some religions call this karma, some psychologists call this natural consequences, the Bible decrees it as, "You reap what you sow." Whatever the source, the idea is the same – there is a direct relationship between what we plant in our minds and what we end up creating.

Thoughts are seeds. They create a garden of feeling in your body. Those feelings can be lovely ones such as happiness or joy or they can be less pleasant ones like fear and doubt. Whether positive or negative, those feelings will create a kind of force field that will attract other energies that are similar. This is one of the reasons the rich get richer and the poor get poorer and why when one thing goes wrong, other things start going wrong as well; our thoughts end up creating energetic fields that begin to have their own powers of attraction.

The trick is to stay conscious of your energetic field at all times. This means staying aware of what you're thinking and feeling.

This morning, for example, I made the mistake of turning on the radio as I waited for the kettle to boil. I don't usually listen to the news first thing in the morning, because I know I'm in a particularly open state at that time. I also have a very clear mind upon waking and usually like to keep it unfettered while I write for a few hours. However, I must have needed a reminder because this morning, without thinking, I just turned the radio on.

As the newscaster recited his news – a list involving more cases of a killer virus that was going around, an update on the severed body of a child that had been found, details of another country building illegal nuclear weapons, I could feel my body reacting. I turned the radio off, but by the time I started work, I was feeling discombobulated. Since I know how important my energy field is to what I create, I decided to do a body scan so I could tune in more deeply to myself and find out what was going on inside me.

Doing a body scan is a great way to check in on yourself. I'm going to describe how to do a body scan because it's such a great exercise for getting in tune with yourself. You can do a short scan to get a quick sense of how you're doing or you can do a longer one for a more detailed description.

> *Start by closing your eyes and focussing on your physical body. Beginning at the top of your head, let your awareness move slowly down your body. Listen and look for sensations, aches, pains, and places of relaxation or tension in your physical body.*

> *(When I did this, I became aware of some tension in my stomach, and a pressure on my shoulders. There was a sort of heaviness in my chest area.)*

> *Now do the same thing with your emotional body. Ask yourself, "What am I aware of feeling?"*

> *(When I did this, I realized I was feeling a bit depressed. It had been raining all weekend so the kayak trip I had planned had been canceled and then a friend had reneged on a get-together we were planning and I was feeling a little hard-done-by.)*

> *The final part of the exercise is to scan your spiritual field. Ask yourself, "Am I feeling connected to my higher powers or helpers?" When I answered this question, it was a big, "No."*

Although I do the scan mentally, I could have drawn it as well, using coloured pens and chalks. Sometimes this makes the experience much more vivid to me.

Once I had the results of my scan, I knew I wasn't in a state to create much of value. I knew I needed to change my energy significantly. There are many tools I could have pulled from my cognitive and energetic kit, but I chose to work with gratitude.

At one time, if someone had told me they were doing a "gratitude practice," I would have smiled, like I might if they'd told me they'd just bought an apple pie. I mean, that's nice, but so what?

Now I know better. Now I bow at the feet of such a practice as if to a spiritual master.

Gratitude is a surprisingly powerful spiritual tool. I think of it as a sort of energetic scythe that can cut down a whole field of deadly nightshade in just a few minutes.

bοω GRΑτιτυδε cRεΑτεs ΑβυΝδΑΝcε

We live in what Buddhists might term a 'grasping' culture. Consumerism propagates to the belief that we need to buy, buy, buy and therefore tries to entice us to do so by projecting image after image of what we should have if we're keeping up with the neighbors. In a consumer society, we're always being told that not only is the glass half-empty, but that if we don't keep consuming, the level of water will deplete until nothing is left.

Whether the glass is half-full or half-empty, gratitude has the power to make whatever amount of water you have feel like a vast lake. It does this by opening your heart to the wonders of your life. The wonders may be small, but that doesn't matter. Practicing gratitude will put you in the vibration of abundance. And in terms of being able to attract more of what you want, that's hugely important. What goes around comes around.

In terms of my own journey that morning, I was still vibrating from the news on the radio, when the phone rang. It was a friend with whom I often walk. Instead of asking me for a walk, however, he told me he was going out on his boat with another friend. More hard-done-by feelings flooded through me. We talked for a while, then said good-bye.

I was intrigued by the fact that this friend had called at this particular time. It wasn't as if we had a walk planned, so there was no reason for him to call. Had my energy field attracted this situation? Wondering this reminded me of the Abraham material which I mentioned previously. Abraham teaches that we create everything we experience. And when Abraham says 'every' experience, he means it, right down to attracting the grumpy cashier at the grocery store. How so? If it had been me in the grocery store, I could have stepped into another checkout line. Or been in the store at another time of day when this particular grumpy person might not have been working. Or if I was in a really great mood, I might not even have noticed the disposition of the cashier at all.

Although there are many times I'd like to deny it, the irrefutable truth is that whatever I have in my life is what I'm in energetic resonance with. That doesn't mean I want what I've attracted or am necessarily even aware of how I actually got it. The fact that I have it may involve patterning passed down from earlier generations, or previous lives if you believe in them, but if I have something in my life I don't want, or don't have something in my life that I do want, part of me is vibrating in energetic resonance with this result.

CHANGING VIBRATIONAL FIELDS

Not wanting my day to continue in the way it was going, I decided to change my vibrational field by giving thanks for all that I was grateful for. As I looked around the room, I felt a swell of appreciation for my house – the beauty of the cathedral ceiling and the lushness of the plants. Then I saw Homer, my yellow labrador, snoring on the couch and felt grateful for him. He's almost 10 years old and I'm aware that I want to appreciate the time I have left with him. Then I thought about my friends and began to feel very blessed to have so many wonderful people in my life. As I did this, I noticed I was starting to feel lighter. It was as if my aura was getting fluffed up. I continued on, giving thanks for my health, my talents and my accomplishments. Then I gave thanks for the air I was breathing, for the sunlight that was streaming though the window, and the trees outside. The colors in the room became brighter. Suddenly the world around me seemed plush and lush.

Gratitude Visualization

Here is a meditation I do for myself or suggest for others when there is a need to increase gratitude. To do it, get yourself into a relaxed place in both your body and mind, then imagine all the people who love you standing in a circle around you. The group of people can also include people who have passed on as well as those who are alive and well. Add in all the spiritual helpers and supporters you have too.

> *Imagine that you can see the spirits of each of these people and as you do, imagine these spirits telling you how grateful they are for you. Grateful not only for all that you do, but for all that you ARE. Feel that gratefulness come out of their eyes and come into yours. Let the feelings this invokes fill up your heart. Go from person to person, drawing all that good energy into your body. If you want to make it feel even more real, imagine that the gratefulness you are receiving has a color, a temperature and a texture.*

> *Move slowly from person to person, until you have completed the circle. When you are done, you might want to thank the group of people for being with you. Then, take a few moments to concentrate on the feelings in your own body. Feed on them for a while.*

When I did the exercise, I imagined that the energy flooding through me had a color. It was warm and golden-silver and washed away any discord, leaving me full of lovely, sparkling warmth.

This is a great visualization to do at any time, but it's particularly helpful if you're feeling dispirited or low. I used to do it for my son when he was little and too agitated to sleep. We'd imagine all the people who loved him and wrapped their loving energy around him like a blanket. He was often asleep before we'd gone around the full circle.

After doing this visualization, I felt as if my inner core had been given an infusion. I could almost feel light shining in the center of my being. The phone rang again. The exuberant voice of my brother came bursting through to my ear.

Exuberant is not a word I would normally use to describe my brother, but it was his birthday yesterday and last week, I'd sent him a package with some birthday presents. He had obviously received them. His demeanor was as airy and happy as a big red balloon. It matched my refurbished mood completely. Was it coincidence that his happy call had come the moment my energy field changed? I don't think so. Because it's long distance and I have a cheaper phone plan, I usually call him on his birthday, but something had prompted him to call.

My brother's gratitude for the present I'd sent him brought even more feelings of well-being into my body. Next year, it will be easy to remember to send him another present. Gratitude has a way of oiling the wheel of abundance. It keeps it moving. Lack of gratitude, on the other hand, will slow down that movement. For example, let's say my brother didn't call and thank me. Would I be likely to send him a gift next year? If I did send a gift, I doubt that it would be sent with the same juicy energy. Or, I might just send him a card. And if he didn't acknowledge that, I might not even do that the following year.

Hearing his gratitude today, however, ensured that I would continue being abundant with him. My abundance will pollinate his abundance, which in turn will pollinate mine and on and on this energy will go. Which is good because gratitude has a very high vibration. That is one of the reasons so many evolved people practice gratitude. They know it has the power to keep them vibrating at a high level.

When we practice gratitude, we become grateful not only for all the people and things Life has given us, but we become grateful for the gift of Life itself. Our consciousness becomes supercharged with the awareness of Life's basic majesty and magic. A majesty and magic that we are not just recipients of, but active partners in creating! So, when we give thanks, we not only affirm the glory of the Master Creator but our own evolving god self as well.

MAKING THE MOST OF GRATITUDE PRACTICE

Here are some suggestions for making the most of a gratitude practice.

- When you are reviewing what you are grateful for, make your gratitudes specific. Instead of saying, "I am grateful for all my friends," say, "I am grateful for Ken. I am grateful for Sallie…" Or, you can be even more specific and say, "Thank you for my friendship with Caroline, or thank you for Kate's caring…" Play around with the language until it feels right for you, but keep the words as specific as possible.

- Let yourself really feel gratitude as you say them. Words carry vibrations and those vibrations have the ability to catalyze a variety of feelings. Those feelings will give your gratitudes juice! So, let yourself feel the abundance you have in your life. Let yourself be touched and moved each time you do them. Choose the words that will have the strongest impact on your heart and feelings.

- Do more than just think your gratitudes. Say them out loud. Or write them down. Involve more than one of your senses. Or, do as Maria Duncalf-Barber, a counselor and workshop leader does – she gives thanks over and over and over again. "I just say them and say them," Maria explains, "until I'm vibrating with their energy. And I say my gratitudes for everything, even the most basic things like my food, my house, my husband. Doing that brings me right into the moment and all that is working for me right now. Then I feel so truly blessed."

- Let your gratitudes fill your heart. The point of this exercise is not to simply make a list, it's to open your heart to yourself and the universe. It's to refresh your knowing that the world is an abundant place and that all you need is out there, ready and waiting for you. So let yourself be deeply moved by your gratitudes. Say them with a full and earnest heart.

- Do your gratutides frequently. Many people do them as part of their formal daily practice, but don't limit your gratitudes to just that time. Say them throughout the day.

- Carry your gratitudes out into the world. You can do this by expressing your gratitude to someone verbally or through a card. There are many wonderful Internet sites that have free cards you can send to people. After I launched my third novel, I sent dozens of these cards to thank people not only for specific work they did on the book, but to all the people who had been emotional supports as well. The cards were full of brightly colored flowers and I imagined them landing on various desktops that day, and the joy they would bring. It was a lovely feeling. People had given so much to me and I wanted to keep those good vibrations moving.

The other reason to send your gratitudes out to the people in your world is that they are hugely nourishing, to both the giver and receiver. Theresa

Sansome, a writer and an artist, put it this way. "It's so easy to be aware of all the little faults our friends or spouses have. When I say my gratitudes, it lifts me above all that. It gets me back on the high road. I particularly notice this in my relationship with my husband, Guy. We have two kids and during the day, most of our interaction is over dirty diapers. But every night, without fail, when we're in bed, we express our gratitude to each other. Doing this gives our marriage so much strength. It makes it vibrant and alive. When I do it, I go back to a place where I hold him in high esteem. It's not like a pedestal, because after a few years of marriage you are totally aware of the downside of your partner, and that awareness can wear a marriage down. But when I do gratitudes for him, I'm consciously choosing to focus on who he is beyond all his liabilities."

• Show gratitude for the way people are, not just for what they do. Send a note of gratitude to someone who showed sensitivity, consideration, kindness or levelheadedness. The more attention you give specific behaviors you want in your life, the more you will get them.

• Have regular gratitude fill-ups. Stop what you are doing a few times a day and tune into all that's going on around you that you feel grateful for. I just did one and here's how I did it. I stopped typing for a minute and noticed the sea blue umbrella outside and was grateful for its color and the gay, summery look it gave my deck. Then I noticed the lovely red stained-glass heart my friend Julie gave me that's hanging in the window and it reminded me of a wonderful holiday I had with her and her partner last summer out on Salt Spring Island in British Columbia. I reviewed some of the lush moments of that holiday and felt even more grateful.

As a result of all the gratitude work I did this morning, I have created a completely different energy field than the one that listening to the radio warped me into a few hours ago. And, what's particularly fascinating to me at the moment, is the fact that I'm noticing entirely different things now that my vibrational state has changed. As you might imagine, there are many things I could notice in the room I am sitting in, but I'm watching how my focus of attention is going to the things that are pleasant. My eyes are actually picking out things that are compatible with my energetic field. I am currently looking at a little clay angel my son gave me for Christmas a few years ago. This angel has a cherubic grin and looks as if he's smiling right at me. He is a special little figure that evokes lovely feelings in me.

Now, just to experiment, I make myself notice other things, like the pile of papers stacked on the floor in the corner. If I were in a more harried mood, those papers would have been the first thing I'd have noticed, not the peaceful angel.

The point I want to make is that there are trillions of things in our world that we could notice at any given time. What we choose to notice, even if that choice is unconscious, is what's compatible or resonating with our energetic field. The maxim "Like attracts like" works even at a perceptual level. So, being a superb custodian of our energy is important. And one of the best ways of impacting your energy field in a positive way is to focus on gratitude.

As Eckhart Tolle tells us in his wonderful book, *The Power of Now*, most of the time, we are living in the past or the future. Yet the present is all we have to work with. And despite how awful life might have been in the past, or might get later on, when I ask people to tune into the present moment, they usually tell me that things are pretty good.

Try it. Take 3 minutes and ask yourself, "What do I have to feel grateful for right now?" Negative thoughts might come up, but gently slide them aside just for the moment and focus on the good stuff. My guess is that you'll surprise yourself at how wonderful your life is right now.

I admit, it's a challenge to practice gratitude when I'm feeling down. When I'm down, I not only don't feel grateful, I'm not even sure I want to feel grateful. That's because when I'm down, I'm in a vibrational state that isn't compatible with being grateful. Obviously, if I'm going to feel better, I'm going to have to adjust my vibrational state. Doing gratefulness practice will do that. If I don't change my vibrational state, I'm simply going to attract more life events that will give me more to be depressed about.

The reason I keep referring to gratitude as a practice is because it's something you can make up your mind to do even if you don't feel like it. Doing it anyway, even when you feel awful, is the only way you're going to feel the full heft of gratitude's spiritual muscle. In fact, the worse off you are, the more powerful the experience will be.

A friend of mine, Diana Wilde, was telling me that when her husband was sick with leukemia, he began a gratefulness practice that changed his energy significantly. Doing a gratitude practice softened him, quelled his upset and allowed him to utilize his own body's healing abilities and the love and help he was receiving from others.

STARTING YOUR GRATITUDE PRACTICE

One way of starting a gratitude practice is to partner with a friend. One person I know talks on the phone with a friend every day for five minutes and they each spend a few minutes saying their gratitudes aloud. Listening to someone else's gratefulness plus saying your own, can create a powerful field for both people involved.

Another way to start is to buy a special notebook and write down your gratitudes. The advantage of having a journal, is that when you're feeling a little less grateful, you can read your other entries and that will change your energetic field in itself.

Also, don't be hesitant to be grateful for the simple things. Thich Nhat Hahn talks about how, when we have a toothache, all we yearn for is to not have a toothache. Yet once the toothache ceases, we forget to be grateful that we are pain free. So don't hesitate to be grateful that you have a bed to sleep in, millions of people in the world don't. Be grateful for the small and unusual – that you are mentally healthy, that you have even a small savings account, that the country you live in is not a war zone. For a staggering number of people in the world, none of these would be true.

Theresa, whom I mentioned earlier, put it well: "When you're grateful for the fact that you live and breathe and have something to eat, the other little dramas that happen in the day get smaller. Before I started doing a gratitude journal, these little dramas used to just take over until sometimes I felt as if my life was one long series of harassing details. I didn't realize this until I heard myself talking to a friend one day. My diatribe sounded like one long complaint. When I do my gratitudes, there is no room for me to do that. I'm too conscious of all the abundance in my life. Then things began to flow again and I felt a sense of happiness and ease with my life. The little problems of daily living couldn't throw me off my center as easily."

SENTENCE COMPLETION

Here are a few sentence completions you can use to plant some seeds of gratitude in your energetic garden. See how they work for you. I find them particularly useful when I am feeling stuck, but they are great to do at any time. Try them out loud right now.

1. I feel blessed to have such wonderful _____.

2. It's easy to feel grateful when I think about _____.

3. It's a good thing I'm so _____.

4. When I express my gratitude, my body feels _____.

5. I feel so lucky every time I think about _____.

6. The thing I'm most grateful for right now is _____.

7. I feel blessed with _____.

8. When I think about what might have happened with _____, I feel truly grateful.

9. When I look around the room, I feel grateful for _____.

10. I feel grateful that life has brought me _____.

PART TWO

CHOOSING, PLANTING AND GROWING YOUR LIFE

Chapter 4

Choosing Your Soul Seeds

"I found that every single successful person I've ever spoken to had a
turning point and the turning point was where they made a clear
specific unequivocal decision that they were not going to live
like this anymore. Some people make that decision
at 15 and some people make it at 50, and
most people never make it at all."

—Brian Tracy

We've spent the first three chapters making your inner soil rich and ready.
Now it's time to plant. What an auspicious moment. What seeds are you
going to sow? There are thousands upon thousands to choose from. How will
you pick the ones that are compatible with your individual climate and soil?
How will you know which ones will bring you the flowers that will make your
heart sing?

As a coach, I encounter many people that, in my opinion, are growing
lives that are too skimpy to nourish them fully. Or they grow lives that fit the
idea they have of themselves, but not their true, soulful selves. Our culture has
some very fixed ideas about what kinds of lives are acceptable and if we accept
these limitations, we can curtail ourselves unnecessarily. What I want to help
you create is a life garden that is full of the foods and flowers that are right for
you and your total blossoming.

A good deal of my time as a coach is spent helping people realign their lives with who they truly are. Unfortunately, there are many people who, in my opinion, are as rare as violets, yet they're trying to be daisies. Not that there is anything wrong with being a daisy. There isn't. I adore daisies. But if that's not who you are, it's only going to bring frustration. A friend of mine has an aunt, for example, who was an accomplished pianist, but in her time, women weren't allowed to have careers, so, after she married, she stopped playing the piano. She accepted the societal dictum prevalent at the time that motherhood should be enough for her, so except for playing a few carols at Christmas, she did not let her hands touch a piano. As if to anesthetize herself from the pain of this, she reached for gin. By the time she was thirty-five, she was hopelessly alcoholic. I can only imagine the copious amounts of alcohol it must have taken to deaden the ache of her life calling.

There is a saying in the Gnostic Gospels that goes like this: If you bring forth what is within you, what you bring forth will save you. If you do not bring forth what is in you, what you do not bring forth will destroy you. Living out our Soul's dream is not some fanciful luxury, it's a necessity for our evolution.

Many books on manifestation and abundance teach people to get in touch with their desires. They argue that desire gets a bad rap in our culture and that we need to acknowledge what a strong and important force desire is. I certainly agree that desire is a strong force. It was strong enough to be the initiating factor in creating your life and mine and it has also been the initiating force in many of our enjoyments and inventions and accomplishments.

To me, the issue is not whether to follow one's desire, the question is which energy center are you going to bring the desire through? For example, when desire is working solely through the second chakra, the sexual chakra, it can lead us into encounters with others that will not foster deeply meaningful relationships. On the other hand, when desire comes through the heart as well as the sexual chakra, a wonderful, life-altering union can result.

So, when you are getting in touch with your desires, see if you can differentiate which ones come from your heart. The heart, especially the sacred heart, is the hub of the entire energy system, processing information from the 3 chakras below and the 3 above. It is the chakra from which our souls can speak most clearly.

James Hillman, in his book, *The Soul's Code*, contends that each of us has a life calling. He postulates that we each have a 'destiny' embedded in us as surely as the design for a magnificent oak tree is embedded in an acorn. If we honor this destiny and help it to flower, then we are acting congruently with the quintessential energy of our souls. As a result, our lives will throng with energy and fulfillment.

Unfortunately, most of us feel pressured to conform to the 'way things are' in the work-a-day world where scant attention is paid to helping us find our true natures. The concept of self-actualisation, although gaining interest, is still considered a psychological luxury and, as a result, many people are living out lives that may be totally out of alignment with their soul destiny.

Inadvertently, the self-empowerment movement has contributed to this by fostering the idea that people can be anything they want. I believe it's true that people can be anything they want to be, one might argue that this is exactly what a significant proportion of our population is trying to do, but attempting to be a day lily when you're a sunflower will not only require a huge expenditure of energy, it cannot bring deep fulfillment. Furthermore, although someone who is off his or her soul purpose may accomplish things, those accomplishments will have no fire – they cannot for they will not be charged with the searing temperatures of the person's inner truth. Actualizing things from your soul takes work too, but soul-centered actions have an intense heat that seems to melt resistance.

When you look at small children, it's often easy to see the qualities of their soul. When my son was born, I was surprised at the strength of his existing personality. He definitely had a presence about him. All babies do. Each child comes in with certain traits and a central nature. That nature may love wild things, or be fascinated with words, or the stars or the theater. Unfortunately, the inherent nature of a child often gets worn down when parents press their reality on that child. John Lennon, for example, lived with a relative who often told him, "Playing music is fine, but you'll never make a living at it." Good thing John didn't listen.

FINDING THE ESSENCE OF OUR DESIRES

Once there was a woman who wanted to create more money. In order to do that, she created pictures in her mind of lots of money passing through her hands. She felt the smooth texture of the papery bills slipping through her fingers, smelled the aroma of the money, she even visualized seeing the denomination of the bills – 50's, 100's, even 1,000 dollar bills. Within a few months, she was able to manifest her dream into reality – but not in the way she expected: she got a job in a bank.

This story exemplifies someone who worked the laws of manifestation but in too limited a way and in a manner that was not congruent with her Soul Self. She wasn't clear about what she wanted and like many of us, started mixing up what I call the 'delivery system' from the event she wanted to have happen and ended up shortchanging herself.

Let me explain this more clearly. If, for example, your desire is to attract more money into your life, take a few minutes to examine what more money would bring. Is it freedom you want? Is it security? Figure out the essence of what you want to create and then see if attracting more money is the best way of attaining that.

Here's an example. I had a client, Bill, who wanted to manifest a Harley Davidson motorcycle. In order to afford the bike, he decided he would take a part-time job to make the extra money. He bought the bike, but soon found himself working so much he didn't have time to ride it. When Bill hired me as a coach, we began talking about who he was on a soul level so he could make sure that what he was trying to create was congruent with his deepest truth. He soon realized that the reason he wanted more money was because he thought money would buy him freedom. Freedom was his desire.

This realization opened him up to explore ways of creating freedom in ways that didn't have such a hefty price tag. Over the next few months, he took up parasailing and delighted in the way it made his heart soar. In the end, he sold his Harley and rearranged his life so he needed less money. Now he works only 3 days a week and the grin hasn't come off his face since.

For this reason, I am always cautious when people tell me they want to attract more money. More often than not, money is just the delivery system and sometimes, trying to create it can send us into realms that are far from the essence of what we desire.

So, go behind your desires to the essence of them and make sure they are aligned with what's in your heart. Desires that are in alignment with the truth that's in your heart are strong and vital. They are fired from the soul and are the seeds of our true selves. In order for our lives to blossom fully, we need to water those seeds and bring them to full flower.

I call these embryonic aspects of ourselves, 'Soul Seeds'. You may know them by their persistence – they often involve desires that simply won't go away despite the admonitions your logical mind throws at them. Or, you may know them by what keeps showing up in your life. When I was a student, I espoused being an atheist, yet I kept attracting people who were deeply spiritual.

The way to find your 'Soul Seeds' is to listen to your Sacred Heart. According to Francisco Rosero, a man who has done a great deal of research in this area, the Sacred (Magnetic) Heart is located in the center of the chest and is different from the physical heart. Because the Sacred Heart dwells in infinity and is the meeting place of both our Spirit and our Soul, it is different from the heart chakra, which functions primarily as an energy processing center. The Sacred Heart is the home of what he calls 'the Divine Spark,' that part of the Creator that resides within us, or the internal 'I Am' of our divine identity.

Rosero contends that The Sacred Heart is the seed pod of who we truly are.

Try this. Take your hand and put it on your chest in that open space just below your throat. This is the home of your Sacred Heart. Pat it gently for a minute to activate it.

Sometimes when people first tune into their hearts, they do so in order to get answers. They want to know, "Should I marry Paul or Susan?" or, "Should I move to California?" This is akin to asking a newborn to give its opinion on what stocks to buy. It isn't fair. If you're not used to tuning in and listening to your heart, the relationship is going to need time to develop and grow. Start with smaller, simpler conversations than those involving larger life issues. For example, try asking this part of you what it would like you to do in the next twenty minutes.

Was your heart able to communicate with you? If not, don't be discouraged. For some, entering the area of the heart will be a bit like traveling to a faraway country – it may take a while to get there and it may involve learning a different language. Some people have relegated their hearts to such remote places, they may have to wait while new communication lines are installed.

If your heart wasn't able to communicate with you, try presenting it with some possibilities. Imagine you are talking to a mute child and watch for even a miniscule response. You might notice a slightly warm feeling after you make a certain suggestion, or a feeling of expansiveness or even lightheartedness.

When I did this exercise just now, my heart had a sort of leaping feeling when I presented it with the idea of doing some yoga and a meditation. I had been working at my computer since very early this morning, so I decided to take a break and do exactly that.

I'm back and in the space of the break, had another idea about how to help you listen to your heart. Try this: remember a time when you were truly and deeply happy. Even if you have to go back to a much earlier time in your life, perhaps a time when you were a child, remember something that made you feel deeply contented. Let the details of the memory be vivid. See the colors that were there, hear the sounds, smell the aromas, remember the texture of the things you were touching – in short, recreate the feelings in your senses. When you have done this, tune into the feelings in your sacred heart.

The feelings may be strong or they may be very subtle. You may experience any of the following:

- warmth
- airiness
- a flooding sensation
- a radiating feeling
- an opening feeling
- joy
- exuberance
- deep gratefulness
- core-filled inner peace

Winning a lottery, or creating some other dream that is not so connected to your heart and soul may feel good, even exhilarating, but it won't give you the same deep satisfaction.

Sometimes when I am coaching people, I will ask them if their heart is happy. The question often surprises people, but they usually know the answer. For example, I was working with a woman a few days ago who had recently quit her job because she hated it. In our coaching call after she'd quit, she was full of doubts.

"Is your heart happy?" I asked her.

"Yes," she said. "I'm scared but I'm feeling good."

"And what does that say to you?"

She laughed suddenly. "That what I'm doing is right," she said. "It's just that my mind is having trouble believing it." She laughed again and I could hear her relax.

As this situation shows, there is often an unexplainable joy when we do what is true for us. Even though doing what is right may be scary or difficult emotionally, our hearts know when we are on track.

Just to flush this out further, take a moment now to remember a time when you felt off course. This doesn't have to be a time when you were in pain or miserable, just a time when you didn't feel you were in the pulse of your heart's truth. Make the memory as vivid as you can, then put your hand on your heart again. What are the feelings now?

The feelings might be subtle again, or they may be strong. Here are some feelings that people report having from this experience:

- an emptiness
- a deadness
- boredom
- resignation
- a closed feeling
- a distressed feeling
- a feeling of weakness

Experiments in Applied Kinesiology have shown over and over again that we each have a truth, and that when we acknowledge that truth and live by it, our muscles respond by testing strong. And when we don't acknowledge our truth or live by it, our muscles collapse and test weak.

Now that you are attempting to communicate with your heart, ask it to speak to you about what it would like you to create in your life right now. If it doesn't answer right away, offer it some possibilities and see how it responds. Don't be surprised if what your heart wants is different from what you imagined. That is exactly what happened to me. When I tuned in, I expected my heart to repeat what it had been saying to me for a while – that it wanted to attract a spiritual life partner. But when I tuned in just now, an entirely new idea presented itself and that was to write a series of books on a variety of healing and transformational themes.

The minute the idea formed itself, my mind began to chew it up, informing me of a variety of reasons why this dream could not be – I didn't know enough, I already had enough work on my plate, who was I to think I could do this? I could feel my heart shrink. Then I thought about Neale Donald Walsch, the author of *Conversations with God* and all the doubts he had when he first began his books. I know I speak for millions when I say how grateful I am that he took his heart's knowing over his mind's advice.

The thought about Walsch made me decide to hold on to this heart's desire. But what about my earlier desire to find a spiritual life partner? Did I need to let go of that? I rubbed my heart as if it were some sort of Aladdin's lamp. A strong heat flooded into my chest. My heart wanted both desires to be fulfilled!!! Both? Wow, could life really get that good? My heart answered by pulsing like the lungs of an opera singer in a full-throated aria.

bEART kNOWING

Sometimes people talk about inner knowing as a kind of gut feeling. When people have a 'gut feeling,' I imagine they are getting information from their second or third chakra. Each of the chakras has wisdom to share, but the wisdom you can access through the Sacred Heart is the wisdom of your soul. Gut feelings are good to listen to and can be helpful in all sorts of business and personal situations, but the truth of your heart is the truth most related to your soul.

Today, many spiritual teachers are telling us to listen to our 'higher self' or 'higher power.' Shakti Gawain, a renowned spiritual teacher, says we are all born into this world with an intuitive guidance system that if we'd been raised in a more enlightened way, we would have learned to follow throughout our lives. Unfortunately, most of us didn't receive much support or encouragement in trusting our own deepest feelings and were often actively discouraged from trusting ourselves and the authority of our hearts.

When I am working with people who want to deepen their relationship with their sacred hearts, I advise them to tune into that area several times a day. I suggest they put their hands there and listen.

Here's another thing to try. Put your hand on your sacred heart area and present it with a scale from 1 to 10, assigning '10' as the number of the highest joy and '1' as the number of no joy at all. See if your heart will pick a number that represents its current state. Sometimes I do this before I head off into an activity or venture, just to get a quick reading on how my heart resonates with this proposed event. I find it a quick way to access its wisdom.

INSPIRED ACTIONS

One of the wonderful things about tuning into the heart is that it will show you the difference between what Abraham calls 'inspired action' versus 'motivated action.' Understanding the difference between these two is important. Inspired action comes from the heart and soul whereas motivated action comes from the mind. We do inspired actions because we are excited about doing them. They involve no push and we usually do them because they feel good, regardless of the outcome.

Motivated actions, on the other hand, usually spring from a sense of unhappiness. We want something to change, so we rally up our energy to DO something. There is usually a fair bit of push in motivated actions as we take something on in an organized and/or significant way. In motivated actions we definitely want something to happen and we put a lot of energy in making that outcome occur.

I have spent much of my life doing motivated actions and know from personal experience how exhausting they can be. Yes, they have brought many good outcomes, but because they weren't fired from the most powerful of my energy sources, they tired me out. And they didn't bring me heart happiness.

When I look back, I notice that I often chose motivated actions when my personal energy field was too clouded with confusion or agitation for me to get a good reading on what my deeper self wanted.

I hear this dilemma expressed by people I work with all the time. "How do I tune into myself and my truest knowing when I'm not in a clear space?" This is a crucial question for often it is when we have a lot 'going on' that we most need to be able to tune into our deepest truth, yet it is at these very times that it is most difficult. The clearing exercises in the Energy Medicine section of Chapter Six will provide you with excellent tools for creating a clean ear for you to listen to your Soul Self.

The other challenge when we have a lot going on is our susceptibility to other people's ideas of what we should do. In times of turmoil or confusion, it's easy to let someone else's enthusiasm about a particular path get us fired up. One of the worst trainings I ever took was The Hoffman Trinity Process. This training might have been excellent for the other people there, but for me it felt damaging to my energy field. When I signed up for it, I was feeling almost desperate to make some changes in my life. This training promised to do that and it delivered, but with a large emotional price tag.

When I look back on this experience, I can see that what I got was congruent with the state I was in. So, now I've learned to attend to my energy field first, before I make a decision. And I want my actions to be inspired, not motivated.

RECOGNIZING SOUL SEEDS

Start by writing down fifty desires. Just let yourself write whatever comes to you, without thinking. When you are done, notice which ones are desires that have been present in your life for a long time, even if you haven't acted on then. Notice which ones originated in your childhood. Underline any that have refused to go away despite all the arguments your mind has made against them.

Ask yourself this question: When I am on my deathbed, will having attained this desire make me feel complete? Or is it something that will seem irrelevant?

Scan your list for the few that make you feel elated in your heart or give you an excited, deep soulful feeling. With your hand on your sacred heart, see if any make you feel downhearted when you imagine not bringing them to blossom.

Now, choose the ones that feel most powerful by your heart and soul.

Write them down.

The Soul Seeds I want to plant and grow are:

1. _____

2. _____

3. _____

Okay, let's get planting!

Chapter 5

PLANTING YOUR SOUL SEEDS

"Our goal is to learn how to align our energy so that we may
prosper and thrive in every area of our lives."
—Elyse Hope Killoran, The Prosperity Partnership

Abundance is a natural energy moving through the universe. Our ability to fully grow that energy, however, depends on our degree of alignment. When we are congruent with who we are and what we want, that alignment gives us a cohesive power to not only attract the energy of abundance, but to hold it for as long as we need to feed ourselves and blossom. When we are not clear about who we are and what we want, the energy of abundance is either not pulled to our particular energy system or even if it is pulled, it ends up leaking out before we have attracted what we want.

If you're like me, you have some idea already about what you want. If you haven't been able to attract that desire to you, that means there are other aspects of yourself – aspects that are usually unconscious – that are out of alignment with those desires. Sometimes it's fear that puts us out of alignment, sometimes it's other emotions, but if you have things you do not want or do not have things you do want, you are out of alignment and need to work on bringing every aspect of yourself into complete congruency.

Carol is a friend who decided she wanted to attract a partner into her life. Even though she wanted this, I noticed that she often talked about the fact that she didn't have a partner. Or she would say things like, "There just aren't any good men out there." It was as if she had 'no partner' written all over her energy field. Of course, the universe mirrored the energetic of that belief back to her and no partner was provided.

When I pointed this anomaly out to her, she decided to turn things around. She began by acknowledging and exploring her fears. When she did, she realized she was terrified to open up to a new relationship. With these fears out in the open, she began to clear them. Using some of the meridian based techniques I outline in the next chapter, she weeded herself of the energy programs that were getting in the way, and planted some new ones.

What occurred almost immediately was that she began noticing that there were good men in the world. Then she started noticing that some of her friends had attracted good men. She was definitely on her way, and I gave her some ideas to speed the process up. The first one she utilized was to imagine she already had her lover in her life. She began imagining him everywhere – she pictured him having breakfast with her, she felt his arms around her, she had imaginary conversations with him – she even bought him a special towel for the bathroom.

Slowly over the next few weeks, I could feel Carol's partner becoming more and more real. It was as if she was 'downloading' him from some huge energetic force. Anyway, he soon showed up in full physicality and he and Carol are now together. Carol says it still feels a bit like a miracle. When we are in alignment with ourselves and the universe, I feel such a 'miracle' is almost predictable. I say this because I believe the universe is a miraculous place. There is really nothing unusual about the miracles. What's unusual is that we live in such times that they are considered rare or imaginary. To me, what's extraordinary is not that miracles exist, but that we've been living as if they did not.

Carol's experience of abundance follows the same format as creating what we want.

- Get clear on what you want.
- Make sure what you want is in total energetic alignment with who you are.
- Act as if what you want is already here and give thanks.

Let's see how this applies to another situation. Let's follow a woman who wants to redecorate her kitchen. At first, Susan thinks she just wants to upgrade the appliances, but as she checks in with her Soul Self and lets her imagination blossom, she realizes that her best dream would be to totally revamp the kitchen and create an atmosphere that is warm and peaceful and nourishing. This was her Soul Self talking and even though she knew she didn't have the money to finance such a large renovation, she let her desire becomes magnetized and full of life.

When Susan had her vision clearly in front of her, she explored the parts of her that were not in alignment with this desire and realized she was worried about spending such a large amount of money. For a moment, she debated with herself and almost talked herself out of going for her vision. She knew a smaller renovation would stress her less financially, but the smaller vision had no juice. It wasn't fired from her soul. And Susan knew the power of visions that are fired from the soul.

Although she didn't have the money, Susan went out and began looking at what she wanted to have in her kitchen. She let her mind spend a lot of time creating what it would look like and she let herself get emotionally excited. Slowly she began purchasing what she wanted.

"I still don't know where the money came from," she says. "From here, there and everywhere, I guess, but I was able to do the renovation far more quickly than I'd ever imagined. I just kept taking one step at a time in complete faith, and it all worked out."

As we can see in both the above situations, Carol and Susan first articulated their desires, then checked in with their souls to see if they were congruent. Finally, they cleared away any emotional dissonance from their vibrational systems . . . the rest was easy.

Donald Neale Walsch in *Conversations With God, Book 3*, describes what he calls the 'Be-Do-Have paradigm' and says that most of us have it reversed. He says that people believe if they 'have' a thing (more time, money, love – whatever), then they can finally 'do' a particular thing (write a book, find a mate, go on vacation, buy a home), which will allow them to 'be' something (happy, peaceful, content, or in love).

According to Walsch, however, 'havingness' does not produce 'beingness,' but the other way around. He suggests that first you 'be' what you want (loved, compassionate, abundant), then start doing things from that energy. He says the universe will fill in the details. When we go to the qualities of 'being' or to what I've described as the essence of what we want, we create a clear template for the universe to respond to. We only have to look around our world to see how excellent the universe is at filling in the details.

CONGRUENCE

We all know people who say one thing and do another. Perhaps they want to be healthy, but smoke cigarettes. Or perhaps they want to attract a new job, but never look in the paper. Wanting something and not following through is like ordering pizza and not giving your address. Or giving the wrong address. The universe, contrary to what some people think, does do delivery, but it needs to know exactly where to take what's been ordered. What I'm encouraging you to do is create an energy field around what you want that is so clear and congruent, it would be like a neon sign that flashes 'the pizza belongs here.'

Susan Smith Jones, who wrote *Abundance Lives Inside of You*, writes that "Spirit can only do for you what it can do through you." We need to open ourselves to the energy of what we want to create fully, to have our entire energetic system congruent with what we want. Then all we have to do is watch how the universe downloads our desires.

Sometimes God responds to us in different ways than we might imagine, as the following story illustrates.

A man was at home when it started to rain heavily. When water started flooding into his house, a rescue truck drove up to take him to safety.

"No, it's okay," he told them. "God will rescue me."

The water got higher and higher and by the end of the day, he was on his roof. A rescue boat came by. Again, he waved them away.

"God will save me," he said. As he was swept off his roof and forced to swim, a helicopter came by, but again, he waved them away.

"God will save me," he shouted.

Eventually the man drowned and when he got to Heaven, he had a meeting with God and demanded to know why he hadn't been saved.

"I tried," God said. "Who do you think sent the rescue truck, the boat and the helicopter?"

The truth is, God, the Universe, Spirit, whatever you want to call it, is willing to give us whatever we want all the time. Through our own confusion, guilt and unconsciousness we get in the way. However, when every aspect of our being is in alignment with what we want to create, then the path to creation is smooth, uncomplicated and swift. Being congruent creates a strong magnetic field that can actually pull in what we want to create. We won't have to do much in the external world because the power of this magnetic force will do it for us. This is law.

On the other hand, if you are only partially congruent, you will have to use more effort, perhaps even resort to struggling, in order to create what you want. If you are totally incongruent, it may be that you won't be able to create what you want regardless of the amount of struggle you are willing to expend.

Do you know if you are congruent? You are congruent when what you want, what you think and feel about what you want, and what you have are the same. The acid test is simply to look at your life and examine what you have created so far. If you have what you want, you are congruent. If, however, there are things in your life, your family or workplace that you want but do not have, or things that you have but do not want, you are not congruent, at least not fully.

In order for you to have something show up in your life, that something needs to be in resonance with what's already in your energetic field. Now, that doesn't mean you have to like what's showing up in your life, but if something is there, there is a match between it and you.

Gay and Kathlyn Hendricks, the famous relationship experts, say that what we have showing up in our world is what we're 'committed to.' They contend that all of us get exactly what we're committed to getting all of the time.

Notice how you respond to this statement. Does it raise some anger? It did in me when I first heard it. You might hear a small voice carping way back in your mind saying, "What the hell do you mean! I didn't want this crappy relationship, or this stupid job or this terrible back trouble!"

But let's be clear. Just because you have something doesn't mean you wanted to have it. It just means you are in energetic resonance with it. Or your energy is committed, to it. Full stop. And the good news is, you can change that energetic commitment.

Julie Henderling and Dr John Parker, of Life Energy Alignment Process (LEAP), talk a lot about this 'energetic resonance' in their work. Energetic resonance is what your energy field is saying, even though you might be verbalizing or taking some actions that are quite to the contrary.

Think of something you have in your life that you would like not to have and ask yourself this question: How might I be unconsciously creating this outcome?

Notice if you feel resistant to this question. Do you want to keep this resistance? If not, there are some exercises you can do to release it, but for the moment just notice it. Just let the resistance be there. Notice how the resistance feels in your body. Notice the grit of it. The barrier of it. The way it slows you down. Now, see if you can let it go. Imagine yourself simply breathing out of your body with your next exhale. Now, drop beneath it and see what's there. What's there is your involvement in creating something you don't want. Is that so terrible to acknowledge? Acknowledgment is the first step to being free of it.

The truth is, we all resist our best choices sometimes. And resisting our resistance is not going to get us out of it. The only way out is through and that means allowing our resistance, seeing the teaching it has for us, then letting it go so we can make different choices.

CONGRUENCY CHECK LIST

Would you like to check your congruency levels? If you have things in your life you do not want or don't have things in your life that you do want, you can expect discrepancies in your congruence. Asking these questions will root out those discrepancies and give you an opportunity to see them in the light. Then you can clear them. But for the moment, let's see if we can uncover them.

To demonstrate the questions more deeply, I'm going to ask them in the context of someone who wants to create a loving, committed relationship. To work them with the issues in your life, insert your own desire in the place of that.

• Am I acting as if I already have what I want? For example, if I want to attract a loving, committed partner, am I acting as a loving, committed partner to myself and to those I love?

• Is there any part of me that isn't loving and committed? Is being loving and committed showing up in every single one of my relationships?

• Is being loving and committed showing up in every thought I have through each and every day?

• What are the payoffs in me not being loving and committed?

• In what ways might I want to stay being unloving and uncommitted?

• Is being loving and committed showing up in each and every action that I take?

• Am I taking actions each and every day to increase the actualization of this loving and committed relationship?

• Am I regularly giving thanks for already having this?

• If God or an angel or a scrutinizing friend were to look at my life, would it be obvious to them what I was committed to creating? Would they see me vibrating in total harmony with what I want to attract?

Once you've done this exercise, see if you can examine the information it revealed in a nonjudgmental way. Be grateful for this information. Most of the time, we carry these incongruencies around with us like concrete blocks and wonder why it's difficult to move forward or more forward quickly. But once you know they are there, you can cut them loose and clear them. Shortly, I will be outlining several techniques and tools for doing just that, but first, let me offer you a meditation.

A MEDITATION ON BEING CONGRUENT

Bring to mind something you dearly want to create. See it out there in the world. Get a strong sensory picture of it, its colors, smells, textures etc. Create it as clearly as you can. Now imagine you are bringing this desire towards you. See it coming into you, coming into your mind, your emotions, your body. Imagine every cell in your body recalibrating with the fact of this desire now being true, now being a part of you. See its existence written on your bones and being sung from every beat of your heart. Become totally at one with the energy of what you desire. Create complete vibrational congruency. Bask in this congruency for as long as you can. When you come out of the meditation, bring the feeling with you. Carry it out into your life with every breath, every word and fill each and every action with its truth.

In my experience, establishing energetic congruence is crucial for creating abundance. It's the next piece in the skill set. Many of us have done the cognitive work, we have known what we wanted to create and even had an understanding about what was in the way, but unfortunately, we did not have the tools for clearing what was in the way. We knew affirmations weren't going to get us there. We knew visualizations weren't going to get us the full distance either. New skills, new tools and technologies were required, but as yet, they weren't available.

When meridian-based therapies came on to the scene, however, we finally had the right tools to complete the job. For me, once I began using them, it felt as if my entire mind, body and spirit moved into a new synchronicity. I felt a deep 'aha' – the kind one gets when the last piece of a puzzle fits into place and the complete picture appears. Then, as if in confirmation, my ability to create abundance moved to a completely new level.

Julie Henderson says, "Once we 'get it' on an energetic level and feel the old, life-depleting resonances shift and release, we can more effortlessly align ourselves with what is life enriching and release the past's hold on us."

She argues that with the right tools, creating big changes is not difficult, certainly not as difficult as we might have thought. To her, healing will simply occur as long as four essential elements are present:

1. Intention to change.

2. Awareness and consciousness. (The focus of most psychotherapy.)

3. Gaining clarity around new possibilities and intentions.

4. Energy modalities to release the old resonance and realign the system with the new intentions.

Luckily for us, these meridian-based therapies have the ability to work with our energetic bodies to create congruency. These therapies have tools that can clear out the old beliefs and install new ones. Whereas most of the traditional therapies work on our blocks and limitations from a cognitive level alone, these newer therapies create a vibrational shift that when paired with cognitive awareness, fire up such a powerful magnetic field that abundance simply occurs. It's as if we move into complete alignment with the forces of the universe itself.

PART THREE

BECOMING A MASTER GARDENER

Chapter 6

WEEDS, BUGS AND OTHER ENERGY ZAPPERS

"Healing is not nearly as complex, difficult and mystical as
we've been taught to believe."
—Julie Henderling of LEAP

As any gardener knows, weeds and bugs and other energy stealers are a fact of life. Although skilled gardeners have enough know-how to create a plenitude of flowers and vegetables despite these life suckers, they are always watching their plants and adjusting water and other nutrients to keep them healthy.

We, as individuals, need to be just as custodial about the health of our own energy fields. And we need to remember that just as blossoming is a natural state for a plant, bliss is a natural state for a person. Children feel bliss all the time. Because they know about the magic and mystery of the universe, they can be enthralled just watching the clouds move across the sky or become blissful seeing the intricate way a grasshopper moves. Bliss goes a lot deeper than ordinary everyday happiness. It's how you feel when you are totally in tune with your deepest self and living in harmony with that self. How much bliss are you feeling right now?

Unfortunately, even though bliss is a natural emotional state, few of us feel bliss at all and usually not for any period of time. Many of us are so spiritually-wilted, we have resorted to living our lives in a mechanistic way, content to just get by. When we move into the energy of attracting abundance, however, we open ourselves to the inherent juiciness of the universe and emotions such as bliss are usually re-experienced. The techniques I am about to describe will clear away any of the energetic debris that is getting in the way of experiencing bliss.

I have drawn some of the techniques from the wisdom of the psychotherapeutic model and some from the field of energy medicine. The first offers wonderful opportunities to increase cognitive awareness, but true healing has to involve more than the mind. True healing has to pervade our entire energetic system. That is where energy medicine comes in.

Until recently, psychotherapeutic modalities have focussed on the mind and the emotions. We are now aware, however, that the mind and the emotions are just two components of a person's energy field. Energy medicine, which is sometimes called 'vibrational medicine,' focuses on that field itself and offers tools and techniques for its modulation. Although most of the techniques in energy medicine bypass the mind, the mind is often in a different state after energy work occurs.

A vibrational medicine proponent, Dr. John Parker, who has developed what he and cofounder Julie Henderling call LEAP, the Life Energy Alignment Process, works as a practitioner in orthodox western medicine. He contends that although his training helps him to find out what's wrong with a patient, it ignores the reasons why his patient is sick. As alternative practitioners have known for years, although orthodox western medicine can cure and even prevent an illness, it does not necessarily heal the person who has it.

The new vibrational therapies include both eastern and western modalities of healing as well as some spiritual philosophies, so they involve the body, mind and spirit. What I appreciate most about them is the opportunity they offer people to tune into themselves and begin to regulate their own energy. Donna Eden, in her wonderful book, *Energy Medicine*, refers to this as a return to 'personal authority.' As she and other energy medicine champions argue, the body is intelligent and has wisdom to impart to us if we're willing to learn its language.

If you type the words "energy medicine" into a search engine, you will be offered hundreds of sites to explore. The burgeoning field of energy medicine is filled with a cornucopia of modalities and tools. The ones I have chosen here, however, are techniques I can personally vouch for. Some involve working with meridians, others access chakras and/or the aura and magnetic field. I have used all these tools on myself and the people I work with. Some seem to be a better fit than others for a particular person or situation, so I encourage you to try them out and see which ones are most helpful for where you are in your life right now. Some are best to do daily in order to keep your energetic garden healthy, others are good for more specific tasks, such as weeding.

I have outlined both cognitive and energetic processes because I believe by working on all levels, we can bring ourselves into a completely congruent state. Use your intuition to find which ones are right for you and try them out – 'workshop' yourself and your life and you will experience how powerfully they will weed out any incongruencies from your mind and energetic system. Using them has created huge results for me and the people in my personal and work world.

Both the cognitive and energetic techniques described below can be self-administered. I have listed the tools in 3 categories:

• Tools for changing your mind and expanding your cognitive awareness
• Tools for opening your heart
• Tools for changing your energy field

In truth, the categories aren't entirely distinct. As most of us have experienced, changing your energy around something will shift your thoughts, and shifting your thoughts will change your energy. Opening your heart will change both your energy and your mind.

TOOLS FOR CHANGING YOUR MIND AND EXPANDING YOUR COGNITIVE AWARENESS

Tool 1: Polarity Work

From the earliest days of its history, psychotherapy has been concerned with dredging the unconscious in order to bring hidden or disowned aspects of ourselves into awareness. When we are conscious of the forces driving us, we are in a better position to moderate our behavior than when we are unconscious.

As anyone who's been involved in a psychoanalytic process knows, becoming aware of unconscious material can take a long time. In my experience, the direct approach involved in polarity processes takes the work to a whole new level of accuracy and speed.

The work of Byron Katie (www.thework.com) and Leslie Temple-Thurston (corelight.com) offer wonderful examples of polarity processes. Byron Katie provides worksheets on her site for people to actually 'workshop' the concepts in a personal way. Temple-Thurston explains some of her processes as well, and although there isn't a worksheet there, she describes her concepts in such detail that it's easy to try them out.

In the next chapter, I 'workshop' some of these concepts through two life situations, one drawn from a situation I worked through with a client and one from my own life. Hopefully, these descriptions will give you a deeper and more experiential idea of how to use the processes and what they might do for you, but for the moment, I want to outline the various processes so you know what they are.

The very essence of polarity work is to explore the 'other side' or the other end of the polarity, so we can bring what's unconscious into our awareness. Thoughts and feelings that we either do not consciously know about, or are not willing to own, are brought out into the open for examination. This creates an expanded and more truthful view of ourselves, and lets us see the areas where we are vibrating differently than we may have imagined. This is vital if we are going to be congruent enough to attract what we want.

One of my clients, a woman named Stephanie, continually railed about her employer whom she accused of never supporting her. Of course, the more she talked about this and gave energy to it, the more pervasive this aspect became. Yes, it was true that her boss wasn't supportive of her, but the way she kept feeding that fact through her thoughts and words, helped it to grow and take on a life of its own. Luckily, she was willing to try an experiment. The first part of the experiment shocked her. I asked her to look at how she was contributing to her boss being unsupportive.

She didn't like this idea and resisted it but when I gently asked her just to play with it, to see if she could find any small part of her that might want the energy of 'unsupport,' she said, to her surprise, "Well, it's funny, but not being supported is what I know. I'm not sure I'd know what to do with someone supporting me."

Now we were on the right track. I encouraged her to explore further and discovered that in her family of origin, when her father gave her 'support' it always came with a truckload of expectations about how she was to perform, so she'd learned to shun it.

Once Stephanie opened herself to being a co-creator to what she had in her life, the healing picked up speed. Because what we give our attention to gains in power and energy, I asked her to start looking for all the ways her boss did support her. She sniffed at this, thinking she wouldn't be able to come up with much, but again, as she opened the doors of her mind, new perspectives breezed in and she was able to see some ways her boss supported her. As she noticed these and then rewarded her boss for doing them, he began to do more!

Within a month, she was feeling very different about her boss.

"I'm retraining him and he doesn't even know it," she told me one day.

Yes, she was retraining him, but she was also retraining herself. So, even when he did things that she previously would have termed unsupportive, she didn't seem to notice as much or be as affected. Because she'd erased her energetic 'hooks' around unsupportivness, his occasional lack of support could not get snagged by her energetic system and just seemed to move right past her awareness and attention.

The fun part for me was that after she recreated her work situation, she was excited about these new tools and began to apply them to other areas of her life. As she took responsibility for what her energy field was creating, and worked on herself, she was able to make other shifts that allowed a new vitality to flood through her.

The truth is, we co-create people. I remember first encountering this truth in an est Communications workshop I participated in at Findhorn. That was the first time I 'got' that there isn't just one 'me' or one 'you.' There are many aspects to each and every one of us and different people bring different aspects to the fore. That's why I might feel confident around one person and less confident around another. It's a co-creative thing.

I remember hearing of an intriguing experiment done by a psychology class somewhere in the United States. Unknown to the professor, the students got together and decided to pay him rapt attention every time he stood near the window and ignore him every time he stood at the front of the class. By the end of term, the professor had been subliminally trained and was regularly teaching while sitting on the window sill of the classroom.

The truth is we all have many aspects to our personalities, any of which can be encouraged at any time. I'm mentioning this because acknowledging that we have many aspects and bringing them into the open is helpful for our healing process. Although we may like to think of ourselves only in terms of our good qualities, it's by owning up to the parts of ourselves that we're less proud of that makes true growth really happen. By owning up to the aspects we don't like in ourselves, we get to see how those aspects are attracting things into our lives we may not want. Only when we do that, are we able to see how we've created what we've got.

There is an exercise in Leslie Temple-Thurston's book, *The Marriage of Spirit*, that exposes hidden fears from the shadow side of our psyches. It does this by asking people to identify something they want, then complete four sentences around that desire.

The exercise goes like this: Fill in the blanks below:

I want .... (insert your desire).

I fear having .... (insert same desire).

I don't want... (insert same desire).

I fear not having... (insert same desire)

Once you have written out the four statements, explore each more fully. Sometimes you'll find yourself really having to work at finding how the statement might be true, and if that's the case, it usually means that you are in a fair bit of denial or that its truth is far from your awareness. I have noticed that when I make it okay for myself to be resisting, the resistance usually dissipates faster and I can find some truth to the statement.

You may find your resistance showing up as an emotion – like anger or indignance – when you contemplate the truth of one of the statements. Or, there may be shame or guilt. Try to accept whatever feelings you have without judgment. They are important clues to what's going on in your energy field.

It is only when you are cognizant of how your energy field is vibrating that you will be able to actively work to change that vibration. Once you are ready to do that, pick any of the techniques listed under Tools for Changing Your Energy Field, later in this chapter.

Polarity work requires ferocious honesty. That honesty, in return, requires compassion, because if you aren't compassionate with yourself, the awareness of these unconscious drives may be too brutal to accept and you might find yourself wanting to abandon the work. And doing this work can change your life. Give yourself a huge pat on the back for doing any of it.

Try out the above technique on an issue you are facing and see what comes up for you. Or, if you want to see how it works, go to the next chapter were I take some real life situations and work them through using this technique.

Tool 2: Questions as Dynamite Sticks

Questions can be explosive. When I get the right one, I can actually hear the way it blasts through blocked thinking. Then, the person will take a big breath and say, "Wow, that's a GOOD question!"

In a way, 'good questions' operate in the same way as the polarity process above in that they flush out the unconscious side of things. Here are three of my favorite ones. Insert them like dynamite sticks into any area of your life where you feel stuck. Or use them with others, but be careful – not everyone will appreciate the blasting power of such questions.

DYNAMITE STICK 1:

How Was I Part of Creating This?

Although most of us say we don't want to be victims, we still find it hard to take full responsibility for being a contributor to what's showing up in our lives. Taking responsibility does not mean that you consciously choose what's showing up. Taking responsibility does not mean you like what's showing up either. Taking responsibility simply means that you are willing to recognize that if you have something in your life you don't want, or don't want something in your life that you do have, there is a part of you that is vibrating or resonating compatibly with that event. This energetic compatibility may have been seeded into your system by your parents or it may have been passed down to you from a few generations back (as research shows, seeds can live hundreds of years). But by unearthing the seeds of weeds and other plants you do not want, you will be able to create a very different life garden.

DYNAMITE STICK 2:

How Might This Situation be Perfect for my Growth?

Again, sometimes there is a lot of resistance to this question. Sometimes people see it as no more than positive thinking, but it is far more powerful than that.

Let me explain through a story. A man who felt his life was being shaken upside down, pleaded with God to make whoever was doing the shaking stop. God answered, "But it's Me who's been doing the shaking."

What if our soul's job is to attract to us exactly the people and situations we most need for our highest and most thorough spiritual transformation?

Francisco Rosero, who has done a great deal of research on the Sacred Magnetic Heart, believes the soul "attracts dramas and lessons to our lives which are necessary to restore harmony to one or more dimensions of consciousness. As we begin to walk along our true spiritual path, the dramas cease and our Sacred Magnetic Heart begins to magnetize synchronicities which accelerate our evolution."

Accepting that a situation is "perfect" does not mean that you become a passive recipient of what life deals to you. It may, in fact, mean quite the opposite, for once we accept the idea that our souls are attracting situations for our best evolution, we might take the nudge and actually embrace these situations and use them to move forward into our highest evolution.

DYNAMITE STICK 3:

What if …

Although I've seen this exercise described in the Abraham/Hick material, it's one I've being doing for years. It can be done anytime and anywhere. I like it because it always expands my idea of the universe and keeps me aware that magical things can happen at any moment.

Most of the time, we use the 'what if…' question in a negative way. We ask ourselves, "What if my partner is cheating on me?" or, "What if I can't pay my bills?" This time, however, we're going to use the question to explode limitations and create new possibilities. We're going to do this by applying the question only to positive outcomes.

The way to do the exercise is to simply ask yourself 'What if…' and add on something wonderful. Here are some examples that I came up with when I was out walking my dog yesterday. "What if I get home and there's a message that someone wants to buy my screenplay? What if S. calls me up and says he's ready to heal our relationship? What if I get an offer to do a workshop at Findhorn? What if my friends are right, that I am totally lovable?"

When I asked these questions, I could almost feel scented flowers growing in the garden of my energy field. They made me feel light and airy and full of possibility. And, I know they will attract what's light and airy and full of possibility.

Tool 3: The God Box

Elyse Hope Killoran used this exercise in her prosperity course, but the idea of it has been around for a while. What you do is find a box or jar and put a slit in the top. Label the container in whatever way you want: God Box, Higher Self Jar – whatever feels right to you. Then, whenever you have a situation that is more than you can handle or know what to do with, write it out on a piece of paper and put it in the container. Allow yourself to let go of all further thoughts or worries about this item. Let God handle it.

TOOLS FOR OPENING YOUR HEART

Tool 4: Gratitude

Practicing gratitude work will open your heart. See Chapter Three for more specific exercises.

Tool 5: Forgiveness

The following exercise was offered by Michael Dawson who, before moving to Australia, was a longtime member at Findhorn. Michael has written two books, his most recent being *The Findhorn Book of Forgiveness*.

As you will discover from Michael's exercise, healing isn't something you have to 'do.' Just as your finger would naturally heal if you cut it, without you having to "do" anything, your emotional and spiritual wounds will also heal when your energy is flowing. Healing is natural and is simply what happens. All you have to do is be open to it. The universe will take care of the rest. In truth, it takes way more energy not to heal than it does to heal. In order not to heal, you have to stop significant life forces. That's not easy. That's why embittered people are so hard. They have to actually tighten themselves up to stop the life force from maving through them.

Doing forgiveness is the fastest and surest way I know to heal the heart. Don't worry if you don't know how to forgive. The process Michael offers in the exercise below will start things moving and as I've said, all you have to do is be willing, the universe will do the rest. And if you're not ready? Or don't feel willing? You can start right where you are and forgive yourself for not being ready or willing. That will get the life forces moving. And those life forces are saturated with healing energy. Just open yourself to it.

ThE AAA FORGIVENESS EXERCISE

Although the words in this exercise are Michael's, I have pared the exercise down to the bones for presentation here. It is a powerful exercise, even in its more succint format. Use this exercise at any time you lose your peace. It utilizes the principles of awareness, self-acceptance and asking for help – the three A's. At one point in the meditation you will be asked to welcome the help that is ever-present for all people all the time, the help we often forget is there. For you this may be your inner guide, Higher Self, angels, Spirit, soul, Holy Spirit, God, Jesus, or the Goddess. I will use the term inner guide but please feel free to use whatever name or term you feel most comfortable with. This symbol represents a presence that is all wise and loving with absolutely no judgment of you. This presence sees what you may call 'sins' as merely nightmares which it seeks to awaken you from. It simply seeks to correct your errors of thinking and return to your memory the beauty of who you really are. It is the self you will be when you totally forgive.

Step 1: Relaxation

Make yourself comfortable and take some slow deep breaths. Tighten and relax various areas of your body, then count backwards from 20 to 1, allowing yourself to become more relaxed as you count.

Step 2: Ask for Help

Send out a prayer to your inner guide in which you welcome and invite its presence to be with you. The help is always there but needs your invitation to come inside. You may wish to imagine this help as a ray of light shining down upon you or as a presence who's holding your hand.

3: Guided Forgiveness

As you proceed through the exercise, don't try to heal yourself. Your job is to invite the healing in by fully accepting your pain and asking sincerely for help.

Step 4:

Bring into your awareness the person or situation you wish to forgive. Allow the feeling to come with that memory.

Become aware of the area of your body where you're feeling tense, anxious, angry, or fearful, etc. Place one or two hands gently over that area. Begin the awareness process by observing the pain: what is its size and shape? Where does the tension start and where does it stop? How deep does this tension go into your body? Does it have a color? Is this area hotter or colder than the rest of the body? Does this area feel hard or soft, or some other texture?

Ask yourself if you want to retain this pain, or let it go. If you are not yet willing to release it, gently accept this fact and tell yourself you can always repeat this exercise another time. If you have decided this pain no longer serves you, and you are ready to let it go, you must take full responsibility for your reaction. Focus entirely on the way that reaction is playing out in your body and gather your intention to release it.

Now, ask for help. Say to yourself, "I am willing to let this pain go. Please help me." This is your call to your inner guide who will respond in a way that is appropriate for your healing. Your job now is to simply relax and trust the process. The healing will happen in its own time.

This is a gentle process; release any sense of urgency. Tell yourself it's OK to feel this pain – encourage acceptance of yourself instead of judgment. Anything you resist will persist, but anything you accept can heal. If you begin to feel a decrease in pain, you know your prayers have been sincere. Just as you chose the pain in the first place, you now choose to let it go. If the pain does not go away, then there is a part of you that still finds it of value. Don't condemn yourself for this, simply do this exercise again at a later time.

As you have experienced in this meditation, forgiveness work is powerful and will release you from the energy that blocks abundance from flooding towards you. I think of forgiveness work as being a kind of Spiritual shower – it will keep your energy field light and penetrable by the forces of abundance.

Tool 6: Listening to your Heart

I described this exercise earlier in the book, but I'll review it here because I think learning to listen to our hearts is crucial in order to attract abundance.

To initiate the process, put the palm of your non-dominant hand on your chest area, just below your throat. When I do this, I find the tips of my thumb and index fingers graze the lower end of my clavicles, the bones joining my shoulders to my breastbone.

Thump here a few times to awaken the energy. To further activate the area, think of some of the people you love. Bring them into your heart and let yourself be aware of what happens to your heart when it is in touch with that loving energy. Sometimes I continue to rub this area while I'm tuning in because it keeps me more aware.

When you feel as if you've made contact, ask your heart to speak to you. Your heart may not be able to respond in words, so watch for images, or pictures, or phrases or feelings. When I did this exercise just now, my heart said it wanted to clear up a recent misunderstanding with a friend. Then it presented an image of a beautiful nature place I sometimes go to and I realized I needed to go there to fill my heart up on the beauty of nature. I made a point of actually going to this place later on in the day and when I was there, I felt my issue with this friend completely resolve itself.

Tool 7: Invoking the Love of God

This is more of a meditation than it is an exercise, but it's powerful. When I recommend it to clients, I tell them to have a pillow available as I find that makes the experience deeper and more real.

Lie down with your arms wrapped around your pillow. If you want to have some soothing music playing, all the better.

Now, imagine that the You that is lying there is God or your Higher Self or an Angel, and that the pillow is the personality you are just now, in this life. See that personality and all its struggles and challenges and allow a God-sized or Angel-sized compassion and love to flow out of you. Let that love and compassion flood down into the personality of You that is being symbolized by the pillow. Say some comforting, loving words as you hug your pillow tight.

When I do this work, I always tell my 'pillow self' that she is safe, that I, as her spiritual self, am going to protect her and be there for her and that I will love her to the end of time. The meditation often brings tears to my eyes and I know when it does that I've really made a bond between my spiritual self and my personality self. Doing it always makes me feel better. So much so, that I think I'll stop writing and do it now. Be back in a little while.

It's now twenty minutes later and I've had some lovely self-loving time. I noticed that as I did the meditation and opened my heart to myself, my heart seemed to open more fully to everyone in my world. I also noticed how the exercise relaxed me. After it, I felt easier about my day and what I needed to create. When I feel loved, I am so much less driven. I can move with the ebb and flow of life with greater grace and ease and have few demands on how things need to be out there.

TOOLS FOR ChANGING YOUR ENERGY FIELD

Tapping Acupuncture Points

The following two techniques, Vibrational Alignment Technique (VAT) and Emotional Freedom Technique (EFT) can achieve life-changing results for a variety of different psychological and emotional concerns. Both involve the tapping of certain energy points on the body and therefore fall under the category of Meridian-Based Therapies.

These tapping techniques provide a kind of emotional acupuncture and adjust the subtle energy field that the physical body is embedded in. This recalibration of the electromagnetic system can create strong and effective results, healing conditions that more conventional therapies have been unable to change.

Both VAT and EFT procedures can be self-administered and are effective with uninstalling fears, anxieties, addictions and other emotional knots, but they are also able to install new beliefs and positive energy with long-lasting results. Try them out for yourself.

Tool 8: Vibrational Alignment Technique (VAT)

Description: Developed by Dr. Parker and Julie Henderling. For a more complete description, go to their web site at www.lifeenergyalignment.com/self.html. My appreciation to them both for letting me write about it here.

How to Do It: Begin by checking your Emotional Intensity Meter (EIM): If you want to get a good subjective indication of the effectiveness of the session, begin by closing your eyes and imagining a thermometer running up your spine. If 10 is a high emotional intensity (feeling strongly, upset, distressed, a strong emotional charge) and 1 is a low emotional intensity (only mild, low emotional charge) what would your current level be?

Gently tap on each point 6-8 times, then hold the point for one deep breath. You can tap on either side of the body and in any order, though working from the top down helps you keep track of the process more easily.

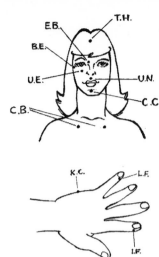

1. TH Top of Head – center top of skull (use whole palm to pat this point)
2. EB Eye Brow – the area where the brow ends above the nose
3. BE Beside Eye – on the side, aligned with the outside edge of the eye
4. UE Under Eye – the flat bony part directly beneath the eye
5. UN Under Nose – between the upper lip and base of the nose
6. CC Chin Crease – in the center, on the chin crease
7. LF Little Finger – on the side next to the 4th finger, at the base of the nail on the cuticle
8. IF Index Finger – on the side next to the thumb, at the base of the nail on the cuticle
9. KC Karate Chop – midway along the outside edge of the hand
10. CB Collar Bone – on each side, in the indentation just below each collar bone curve (place index finger in the center hollow, then move about 1.5 inches to each side)

Begin patting firmly on the top of the head and say:

"It's only natural that I have this (say the feeling) but I am ready to let it go now."

"I desire to be free of this (say the feeling) and I am ready to let it go now."

Continue tapping using two or three fingers (6-8 times on each point) on the rest of the VAT points.

TIP: To make the process even more effective, after each point has been tapped, pause and hold the point, then take a deep breath in through the nose and out through the mouth. Then continue to the next point.

Unlike traditional affirmations, we actually *want* to focus on the negative feeling for the duration of the tapping, in order to pull it up and out of the energy system. If you become upset or feel a brief intensifying of the feeling, this is a sign that VAT is working on a deep level. Once you've done the sequence, recheck your EIM, Emotional Intensity Meter.

If the intensity has not come down to a low number or zero, you may need to do one more round, or identify another closely related emotion that is still resonating, and then tap for that feeling. Often there are a number of emotions at work together and each must be pulled as a 'separate weed.'

This is far more powerful than traditional affirmations which work only at a cognitive level. All the intellectual understanding in the world does little if your energy system is lit like a 'neon sign' and radiating a different message than what you are asking for. By focusing on the positive feeling while tapping, you literally 'install' it in the energy system.

Identify the positive feeling you want to 'install' and begin patting firmly on the TH point while repeating the following statements:

"It's only natural that I have not been feeling (say the positive feeling) but I am ready to feel it and experience it now."

"I deserve to feel (say the positive feeling) and I am ready to feel it and experience it now."

Continue with your finger tapping (6-8 times) on the rest of the VAT points (in order from the top down is recommended) while repeating:

"I am now feeling (say the positive feeling)."

Emotional Intensity Meter (EIM): You can now recheck your EIM and hopefully feel an improvement

What You Can Use VAT For: Fears, phobias, installing new beliefs, uninstalling old ones.

Other Considerations: On the web site, Julie talks about the importance of starting a tapping session with some sort of objective means of assessing the intensity of your feelings. She uses her own fear of snakes as an example, saying that before she began tapping, she wasn't able to even look at a picture of a snake without a big reaction. She determined that being able to look at a picture of a snake would be her test of whether the tapping had diminished her fear or not.

Having an objective measurement is important for both VAT and EFT. When I first used it on my fear of heights, I imagined myself at the top of a building looking down and then assessed that level of fear at 8 out of 10. Then, after I did a round of tapping I was able to test that same image. My EIM had dropped from 8 to 2.

The other thing that's important to remember is to tap for all facets or nuances related to the issue. For example, if you were working with uninstalling a fear of snakes as Julie was, she needed to tap on every aspect of what frightened her: the suddenness of seeing a snake, the look of the skin, the way they slither, her fear of being bitten, etc. Also, it's important to tap on all the scary memories so every trace of the fear energy can be uninstalled.

Julie suggests you continue to tap until there is no resonance of the fear whatsoever. She reports that she was able to completely eradicate a lifelong terror of snakes in just under an hour. She is now living in the country and often encounters snakes in her garden, but all signs of the phobia are gone and she is left with nothing more than a "healthy desire to keep away."

Tool 9: Emotional Freedom Technique (EFT)

Description: Dr Roger J Callahan, a psychologist with over 40 years of experience, has been teaching a technique that one of his students, Gary Craig, developed into what he calls, EFT, the Emotional Freedom Technique, which he says is as important to psychology as the Salk vaccine was to polio.

How to Do It: Like VAT, EFT also involves tapping various points on the body, but EFT adds in some humming, counting and eye movements. A comprehensive description can be found on Gary Craig's site (www.emofree.com), as well as a free comprehensive manual that can be downloaded.

Considerations: As with VAT, there are some important considerations to be aware of with EFT that will enhance its effectiveness greatly. I discussed some of these in the VAT section. For a far greater description, go to the web site.

What You Can Use EFT For: To clear out any unwanted thoughts, emotions, phobias, addictions and ill health. It can also be used to "install" any new thoughts, beliefs or emotions to foster renewed health. Although either of the above tapping procedures can "seed" a new outcome, I use VAT when I have less time and the feelings aren't too intense, and I use EFT when the job needs something more comprehensive. I may be partial to EFT because it was so helpful when I was working with a fear of flying. Particularly flying in helicopters.

My fear of helicopters had been installed when I was a child and had been with me a long time. Because of its history and strength, it was hard for me to believe that such a fear could be obliterated easily. Anyway, a few days before the scheduled event, I began doing EFT, making sure I tapped for all the stimulating aspects, e.g., being up high, twisting and turning in the air, seeing the ground way below, etc. When I did go up in the helicopter, I only had some minor anxiety which, interestingly enough, was related to an aspect of the flying I hadn't tapped for (the way the helicopter can drop in the air). When it wasn't dropping, however, I actually enjoyed the ride. This proved to me, without a doubt, how powerful these techniques can be.

Tool 10: Temporal Tapping

Based on the Energy Psychology work of Dr. Fred Gallo (www.energypsych.com). The temporal tap is another way to incorporate positive beliefs and to eliminate negative ones. In right-handed people (and most left-handed people), tapping the left side of the head, just in front of the opening to the ear, then continuing to tap the area on the head up and around the ear to the back. This is the Temporal Sphenoidal (TS) line and tapping it causes acceptance of positive statements/beliefs (e.g., I am worthwhile), while tapping on the right results in acceptance of "negatively" stated positive statements (e.g., I am not worthless). This pattern may be reversed in some left-handed people. It appears that the TS line is related to the location where the bodymind filters incoming sensory information. By tapping at these locations, the filtering system is temporarily disengaged to allow the assimilation of positive messages.

How To Do It:

1. Identify a belief, behavior, etc. that you want to change. This may be related to negative core beliefs concerning self-worth, unwanted behaviors, physical health problems, etc.

2. Develop both positive and negative phrases in the present tense regarding these beliefs. For example, "I am worthwhile." AND "I am not worthless."

3. Tap firmly with the finger tips along the RIGHT TS line from the

front to the back of the ear while repeating the NEGATIVELY stated desired belief. Examples: "My heart does not beat at an unhealthy irregular rate." "I dislike smoking."

4. Tap the LEFT TS line from the front to the back of the ear while repeating the POSITIVELY stated desired belief. Examples: "My heart beats at a healthy regular rate." "I enjoy being a non-smoker."

5. Repeat the treatment daily for several weeks.

Tool 11: Thymus Circle

Description: This exercise, developed by Dr. John Diamond, works on stimulating the Thymus gland, which provides life energy support and immune capability.

How To Do It: Bunch the finger tips of the right hand together and hold over the thymus area, which is at the center of chest, just above the breast area. Breathe deeply and slowly in through the nose and out through the mouth three times bringing all of your awareness to the thymus gland. Tap rapidly in an anti-clockwise direction forming a circle around the thymus area while saying out loud the positive statement you wish to align with.

What It's Good For: Boosting the immune system, boosting life energy, installing a new belief or emotion.

Tool 12: Tarzan Tapping

Description: This is a quick 4-step process, developed by Julie Henderling and Dr John Parker, which will recalibrate your energy system so it's resonating with life-enhancing beliefs rather than life-depleting beliefs.

How To Do It:
1. Write down a belief you want to release. While saying, "I now release, from every cell of my being, the belief that ...." (insert what you want to release) and tap heartily on both sides of your chest like Tarzan. Tapping on these areas is stimulating the K27 acupuncture points.

I used it just now on myself to release the fussing I'm doing about a certain relationship. So I said, "I now release, from every cell of my being, the fussing I am doing in my relationship with W."

2. Take three long, deep breaths.

3. Write down the new belief and begin tapping the top of your head, near the center (this is the powerful Governing vessel 20). For me, this was, "I now relax into my relationship with W."

4. Take three long, deep breaths. You can repeat the process if necessary.

TOOLS FOR GENERAL ENERGY ENHANCEMENT

Tool 13: The Thinking Cap

Description: From the Brain Gym processes, this exercise will clear blocked energy and create mental clarity by stimulating the multitude of minute acupressure points in the ears.

How To Do It: Working both ears at the same time, starting at the tops, massage the edges of the ears and pull the edges out as if unrolling them. Work your way down to the base of the lobes and back up again. Pause and breathe and connect with the change in your energy state.

What You Can Use It For: To recharge your energy when you're feeling tired and to create clear thinking.

Tool 14: The Three Thumps

Description: These come from Donna Eden's work and are a wonderful way to energize and boost the immune system.

How To Do Thump A: Move one hand down your throat to the "u" in the bone at the base of your throat. With the fingers of each hand, follow the bones each way to find the little bump to either side. Drop about an inch down from that notch and then slightly outward until you feel a small indent. These are the K-27 points, which affect so many of your energy pathways. Firmly tap/massage them for 30 seconds.

How To Do Thump B: Move your fingers a couple of inches down from the K-27 points into the center of your sternum or breastbone. This is your thymus point. Tap vigorously for 20 seconds.

How To Do Thump C: Move your hands a few inches directly down from your nipples to the rib. Using all your fingers, thump this spleen point for about 15 seconds.

TOOLS FOR CHANGING YOUR ENERGY IN ADVANCE

Tool 15: Intentioning

In the Abraham/Hicks material, this is called 'prepaving,' but I like the word 'intentioning' better. As I mentioned in Chapter One, setting an intention acts like a compass, keeping us on track for accomplishing a goal or bringing about a desire. To make the full use of the power of intention, take a moment before an event or situation to consciously 'set' how you want to be, then recalibrate your energy field so you are in alignment with that intention. Here's an example. Let's say I have a meeting scheduled for later on today that I'm feeling tense about. What I can do is set an intention, not on the outcome, because we can't determine how other people are going to act, but on how I want my energy field to vibrate both during and at the end of the meeting.

I set an intention to be calm regardless of what happens in the meeting, then imagine the meeting, imagine handling certain people and situations, all within this calmness. I can even imagine something tricky being thrown at me and create the intention to handle that situation well. I did this when I was intentioning a great birth experience before my son, Jason, was born. Every day while I was pregnant, I saw myself having a wondrous experience, handling the entire experience easily and joyfully. I even imagined some 'difficult' energy coming my way, although I couldn't know in advance what that might be. When something difficult did happen in the delivery room, I was totally prepared.

"Ah, there it is," I was able to say to myself when it happened and immediately modulated my energy field to stay calm. I learned later that a friend of mine had a similar situation arise in her birthing process, but she wasn't prepared and reacted negatively in such a way that her entire birth experience was affected. Intentioning might have saved her from that.

I have found the tools listed above to be extremely helpful in recalibrating my energy field and the fields of others I work with. They are quick and effective and elegant. Get to know them. The more you use them, the more effective they will be.

Chapter 7

THE TEACHING OF THE COMPOST HEAP

"You're the one! You are your own freedom. Marry yourself.
You're the one you've been waiting for all your life.
You are your own happiness. It's all inside you."
—Byron Katie, *Loving What Is*

The wonderful teaching of the compost heap is that however bad things in your life garden get, however many dreams die or get overpowered by weeds, everything can be 'recycled' to create flowers to come. This happens in the natural world all the time – things break down or decompose, then reorganize and grow again. Many gardeners take advantage of this process by creating a compost heap.

In my town, not many people compost. I have a bin outside my door for all my fruit and vegetable scraps, but I know I'm the exception. In North America, creating garbage is a way of life and an entire industry has grown around it. Unfortunately, the same mindset that creates physical garbage, also creates emotional garbage. I know a man, in his 30's, who has had many sexual liaisons. He consumes women and then tosses them away. Many of the women he has been with have been hurt from knowing him, others are on their way to being hurt. I know he hurts others because inside, he is hurt, so I have compassion for him, but I still want him to clean up his act. I want us all to clean up our acts. How many people have you been hurtful to?

In my own world, there was a time when I created some 'emotional garbage.' Although I can't change what I did, I have done my best to go back and make reparation. I also have a clear commitment to live my life cleanly, taking complete responsibility for what I create. And I recycle everything I can, both physically and emotionally.

Wouldn't it be wonderful to create a life that left only blessings to those who knew you? Even though that may be a lofty goal, only obtainable by a few, it is possible to compost our emotional material so it can be turned into soil rich enough to enhance ourselves and our relationships.

The energy techniques described in the last chapter will get the composting process started, but in this chapter, I want to show you how to use the tools more specifically by taking you through a real-life situation or problem (if anything can ever be considered a problem in this new paradigm).

Daily Practices: Before I go through the procedure of composting a particular problem, however, I want to talk about how to set up a practice for keeping your energetic garden clean on a daily basis. Although I have been meditating for years, since I have discovered the tools of energy work, I use them every day to check in on myself and assess the state of my energy; to clear away any debris currently in my system; and to recalibrate myself so I'm operating at full energetic vibrancy.

My daily routine involves four parts:

1. Body Food

I start with a short session of yoga and/or stretches to wake up and energize my body. Then I do the Three Thumps as described in the last chapter.

2. Creating Sacred Space

After the movement portion of my routine, I get my meditation cushion and light a candle or put on music. Then I go inside myself and align with my highest good and ask my helpers, any special angels or elementals as well as my deep inner wisdom to be with me. I then say my gratitudes and feel them with my heart.

3. Inner Attunement and Recalibration

Once I have my helpers in place, I scan the energy field in and around my body. This field, in my awareness, feels egg-shaped and extends a few inches to a few feet (depending on how I'm doing) around my physical body. I scan the outside perimeter of this energy field, or what you might call the 'skin' of my aura. When I first began doing this a few years ago, I was amazed at how thin this protective skin felt in some areas around my body. In fact, in some places I couldn't feel it at all. This makes complete sense to me now, as at that time in my life, I don't think I had a cohesive energy field and certainly did not have a strong healthy boundary that said, "This is me." Back then, it was not uncommon for me to feel invaded by life events. I felt totally penetrable from outside forces and often felt exhausted by other's people's stuff. When I began to do energy work on myself, all this changed.

If, during this scanning routine, I feel a repair or strengthening is needed, I will begin wrapping energy around my body in that area, in the same way a caterpillar might wrap the strands around its cocoon. I usually feel myself gaining strength the moment I do this. It's as if I've stopped up the leaks and now have an energetic container to fill with my own energy.

Once I have completed this work on the skin of my aura, I begin working on the energy inside the skin. I do this by imagining a clock sitting face up on each of my seven energy centers or chakras. If a particular chakra doesn't feel healthy or vibrant, I move my hand counterclockwise to clear out the unwanted energy, then move my hand clockwise to strengthen it.

When I have finished adjusting each of the energy centers, I do an energy wash (which I described in Chapter Two). I imagine waves of energy coming into the top of my head (the crown chakra), and see them washing down into my body. This is a variation of a meditation I learned at a Buddhist retreat many years ago and I've done it ever since. I usually give these waves of energy a color – often gold or silver – as I visualize them streaming through my mental body, my emotional body and my physical body. If I feel there's an area that needs more attention or healing, I let the energy pool there.

The Spiritual Wash recalibrates my energy and realigns me into a cohesive whole. When I feel myself thrumming, I imagine sending the energy out, seeing it extend out to all the people in my world, healing them in the same way it's healed me. I also send everyone unconditional love and acceptance, making sure I include those people I am having a hard time being loving and accepting towards. I then release the energy so it moves out even further, going to all living things. To complete, I imagine the energy washing back over me, flooding me with the same energy that is going out, in a vast energetic circle.

4. Healing a Specific Issue

If I have an issue or I'm trying to heal an emotion like anger, or hurt or fear, I will usually focus on it in the moment, offering it to my deepest knowing and to my helpers. This is the time I might do some VAT or EFT to clear anything that needs clearing or install some new energy or belief. Then I set my intentions. Once they are in place, I take a few moments to make sure my entire energy field is calibrated towards this intention. This might involve another round or two of VAT or EFT or other energy medicine tool. When that is done, I move on with my day.

DEALING WITH BIGGER ISSUES

Of course, even with this daily routine, issues sometimes arise that require special attention. Below are some examples of how the tools and techniques I have already described can be used to create deep and comprehensive healing.

To make this as clear as possible, I'm going to use the example of John, a man I used to coach, and show how, using these tools, he was able to make one of his Soul Seeds blossom.

When John first called me, he was already clear about what he wanted: to find a life partner. His marriage had ended a few years ago and he felt he was ready to get involved again. He had made a few attempts to date, but nothing seemed to be happening.

In talking to him, it was clear he knew what he wanted and that his desire came from a place of truth inside him, but something was getting in the way.

To find out what, I suggested he do some polarity work. I wrote down the following four statement and asked him to fill them in.

> *A. I want.... (insert desire)*
>
> *B. I fear.... (insert desire)*
>
> *C. I want....(insert opposite desire)*
>
> *D. I fear ....(insert opposite desire)*

His answers looked like this:

> *A. I want to find a life partner.*
>
> *B. I fear having a life partner.*
>
> *C. I want not to have a life partner.*
>
> *D. I fear not to have a life partner.*

Once John had done this, I asked him to elaborate each of the statements. His answers looked like this:

> *A. Why I want to have a life partner:*
>
> *Companionship*
>
> *Spiritual growth*
>
> *Sensuality*
>
> *Feeling more loved*
>
> *Share financial commitments*
>
> *B. Why I fear to have a life partner:*
>
> *I'm afraid I'll get hurt. Again!*
>
> *I'm afraid I'll hurt someone else.*
>
> *I'm afraid my life will go crazy again.*
>
> *I'm afraid I'll be needy.*
>
> *I'm afraid I'll feel inadequate.*

C. Why I want not to have a life partner:

Life is simpler on my own.

I can take care of my own needs.

I can do my own thing.

I am not dependent on anyone for love.

I'm not on a roller coaster of emotion.

D. Why I fear not having a life partner:

I will have given up on something important to me.

I will end my life not knowing how to do good relationship.

I will prove once and for all that I'm unlovable.

John found these answers surprising. "I never realized I was so mixed about having a relationship," he said. I smiled. To me, the fact that he hadn't already manifested what he wanted, had been ample demonstration of his mixed energetic.

Since John seemed open to exploring further, I asked him whether his recent actions to find a relationship were in greatest alignment with statement A, B, C or D. He answered 'C' (not wanting to have a life partner) because he said he hadn't really done much to attract a relationship other than wishing for one.

Then I asked him which statement his heart was in most alignment with. He said, 'A' (wanting a relationship) because he knew having a relationship was his heart's strongest desire.

My next question was "Which statement is your body in most alignment with?" Since his stomach got butterflies in it at the thought of having a relationship, he said 'B' (fearing a relationship) that his body was most congruent with being in fear of having a life partner.

When I asked him to tell me which statement his thoughts were in greatest alignment with, he said 'A' (having a relationship) because it was something he thought about all the time.

My final question was, "Which statement does your soul resonate with?" To that, he answered, 'A' (having a relationship).

John's answers showed a variety of energetic dissonances. His heart was vibrating, "Yes, I want a relationship," but his gut was saying, "No, I'm too frightened" and his soul was worried he'd never get over his fears and get on with creating one. The result was an energetic knot. No wonder he wasn't getting anywhere in attracting a partner. Even if his intention had been strong, it was unlikely, given his inadequate state of energetic alignment, that he would have been able to make one happen.

It was Carl Jung, I believe, who said that fate is the unconscious playing itself out. As long as John was unaware of his conflicting energies, he was fated never to have his desire. But once he realized that the reason he wasn't actualizing his desire was due, not to fate, but to his unconscious energetic field, he could change that field and create new outcomes. As you will, too.

Now that John and I knew what we were up against, it was time to come up with some action strategies that would bring his energetic system into complete alignment. Here is a list of the possible action steps I developed for John to consider.

He could:

- remember all the wonderful times he'd had with past lovers. When a relationship ends, if it ends painfully, it is often that pain which is fresh in our minds. But even the most painful relationship had lush and lovely times at the beginning. Even though we are sometimes reluctant to go back and remember those good times, it is crucial to do so if we are going to attract something lush and lovely in the future. Remembering the good times will create the kind of positive energy field you're going to need if you are going to attract a positive new energetic. It's the old rule: like attracts like. I can't state this strongly enough.

- utilize meridian-based therapies such as VAT and EFT to clear old wounds and plant new life-affirming statements. He could even pick some of the comments he'd made from the four statements and uninstall them: e.g., since he'd owned up to being frightened of having a lover because of fears he might get rejected, he could uninstall this belief and install, "I am now ready to be accepted in a relationship."

- write down some healthy, new boundaries for himself so he was sure that the next person he let into his life would be a healthy person for him to be involved with.

• decide to hand the entire issue over to God by creating and using a God Box, as described in the previous chapter.

• ask his spiritual knowing, angels and/or guides to bring the perfect partner to him.

• prepare the way for his new life partner by imaging her in his life in every way and giving thanks.

John chose to take all of the above action steps, but once I taught him EFT and VAT, he focussed on those, tapping out the fears he identified when he elaborated on the four initial statements and installing new beliefs that would counter his fears and allow him to create a new and different life. John had only been doing this clearing work for a short period of time when a new woman came into his life. Whether this woman will be his life partner is still to be determined, but so far, it's looking good. The relationship is bringing up issues for him, but instead of being daunted by these issues, he's seeing them as opportunities to complete what he's calling 'his inner renovation.' Meanwhile, he's having a great time.

So, that's John's saga. And now, here's one other example of working a 'problem' through, this one drawn from my own life. In this example, I implement some of the other tools I described in Chapter Six.

A few years ago, I was in a relationship with a man named S. that ended hurtfully. I had been living with this hurt for a while and finally decided it was time to heal it. I started the healing process by doing the polarity process as above. Here's what I came up with.

> A. I want a healed relationship with S.
>
> B. I fear a healed relationship with S.
>
> C. I want an unhealed relationship with S.
>
> D. I fear an unhealed relationship with S.

Once I had the statements, I fleshed each of them out more fully.

A. I want a healed relationship with S.

Healing this will help me to move on more fully.

If I heal it, maybe we could be friends. I miss him. (That was a surprise.)

I don't want something to have the better of me.

B. I fear a healed relationship with S.

(I notice this feeling is harder to find so is probably more unconscious for me.)

Healing it would mean being ordinary again. Right now, I'm still special or imagine I am even if it's just as an unresolved past relationship.

Healing the relationship would mean I'd have to finally let it go.

C. I want an unhealed relationship with S.

Things can stay the same. I need do nothing
I can keep blaming him for everything.
I don't have to look at what I did.
I can keep walling him off.

D. I fear an unhealed relationship with S.

If I don't heal it, it will always feel like a failure.
I will have to continue carrying this hurt.
I am bigger than this. Not cleaning it up keeps me small.

After doing these four statements, I asked the same questions as in the previous situation I used as a working example.

Are my actions in greatest alignment with A, B, C or D?

Since I had done nothing to heal the relationship with S., I had to answer, 'C' (I want an unhealed relationship).

Is my heart in greatest alignment with A, B, C or D?

I answered 'A' (I want a healed relationship).

Are my feelings in greatest alignment with A, B, C or D?

I answered 'B' (I fear a healed relationship).

Are my thoughts in greatest alignment with A, B, C or D?

I answered 'B' (I fear a healed relationship).

Which one does my soul resonate with?

I answered 'A' (I want a healed relationship and would lament an unhealed relationship).

Like John, my job was now to turn off all the resonances that were not in alignment with what my Soul knew was right for me. I started by reminding myself of all the wonderful times S. and I had paddling, skiing, skating and talking as we walked with our dogs. It surprised me to feel such a flood of warm feelings at these memories.

Softened by these memories, I began to do 'the work' as described by Byron Katie on her web site, www.thework.com. Her web site describes a method for working through judgments and creating what she calls 'turnarounds.' (You can do the process online or download the worksheet, it's a very usable site.)

The first step in the process is to write out what's got you upset and how you think the other person screwed up. As I answered this question, I knew that my biggest gripe with S. had been his unwillingness to commit to our relationship and his subsequent dropping our friendship when the lovership was over. I wrote out all my feelings and thoughts and I wrote out all my thoughts about what S. should have done and how he should have been.

The next step in the Katie process asks you to answer four questions, each of which challenges our perception of how we think things are. As I deeply questioned myself about whether what I had imagined S. doing (abandoning me) was actually true, I was amazed to see that although I had accused S. of dumping me, I had abandoned myself long before he did. Most of our time together was spent at his place, with his friends, doing the things he wanted to do. And when he said he didn't want to have the kind of relationship I wanted, I told him that wasn't okay with me. I withheld my love for him and my friendship from him just as I had accused him of doing.

I could almost hear the 'splat' of my projections falling from the screen of S. to the ground at my feet. What a revelation!

Although I have only described the Katie work superficially here, when

I worked the process deeply, it shifted my perception of S. and created what she calls 'turnarounds' that changed my whole idea of what had happened. I could feel my entire chest open as the hurt I had held towards him softened and began to leave my body.

Now that I had the cognitive understanding, I did some EFT work to finish off the rest of the healing. I could have utilized energy tools like EFT first, but I find it helpful to have an intellectual understanding of how I set things up emotionally so I can see my patterns and work with myself in a more preventative way.

I 'tapped' through a release of any remaining hurt from S. and then tapped in how totally loved I am. After I was vibrating with this feeling of being loved, I invited S's face into my imagination and sent him love and forgiveness and asked for love and forgiveness in return.

I can truly say that if I saw S. now, my feelings for him would be entirely different. I feel cleansed of my hurt and grateful for the many wonderful times we had. I feel freed up and indeed I am for none of my energy is knotted into this old wound anymore. In fact, I wouldn't even think of it as a 'wound' now. The word 'wound' is part of the vernacular of the old way. There are no wounds in the new paradigm. Just as there are no old weeds in a compost heap. For when we recycle, even the hardest of feelings decomposes, then recomposes to make new energy we can use for living more fully right now.

Rechecking Alignment

As you work with the tools, you'll find that some of them work better for you than others and some will work better at certain times than others. That's just the way it is. There is no right way for everyone. Or no right tool for every occasion. Experiment and see which ones work for you at what times. You can recheck your energetic alignment as you go and see how successful you are being about clearing the old dissonances from your energetic field. Here are some of the ways you can do that.

Look at What You're Creating

Of course, the best and surest way to test the state of your energetic field is to look at what starts to happen in your life. When you move into vibrational alignment, the universal forces of abundance will start to flood through you and things will begin to happen. Forget what you have created, look at what you are creating right now. This moment is the only moment you have. Are you in a state of bliss? Is the magic of the universe thrumming through your body and soul? If not, how about creating that?

CHECK YOUR VOICE TONE

Maybe it's because I have a strong audio sensitivity, but listening to my own voice tells me a lot about my energetic state. If my voice is deep and low, I know I'm tuned into my deeper self. If it gets high or thin, I know my energy field is beginning to get stressed. Think about the last time you had a luscious lovemaking session – do you remember how your voice sounded afterwards? It sounded this way because you were deeply relaxed and happy and at peace. What would you have to do to have your voice vibrate through you in the same way right now?

The voice can provide continual audio feedback. Get to know it well and it will tell you all you need to know.

PICK A NUMBER

Sometimes, you can just ask yourself, "How congruent am I with what I want?" and pick a number between 1 and 10, '1' being the least congruent and '10' being the most congruent. Very often, this simple technique will give you a quick assessment of your energetic state of alignment.

MUSCLE TEST

The body has its own wisdom and truth. According to kinesiologists like David Hawkings, author of the fascinating book, *Power versus Force,* muscle testing is one of the most effective tools an individual can use to access deep inner truth.

There are many books that outline how to do muscle testing, but most involve the necessity of having someone else at hand to do the muscle test on you. Julie Henderling offers some techniques that you can perform on yourself which she describes in her new ebook, *Accessing the Amazing Power of Your Inner Guidance System through Energy Resonance Checking* (available at her web site, www.lifeenergyalignment.com.)

One of the methods she describes that I particularly like is called Finger Checking. Here's how you do it.

Finger Checking

Before you do any sort of muscle test, you need to set up a clear understanding with your subconscious mind about what is Positive and what is Negative. Julie Henderling uses the term ON for a positive resonance and OFF for a negative resonance which I like, because it allows me to test whether certain energies are operating or not.

Generally, muscles hold firm or are ON when there is something positive or true happening. Conversely, they collapse or feel weak, turn OFF, when something is not true, or is negative. To ensure that this understanding is pervasive through your system, think of a statement that is an unequivocal ON for you. For me, if I say, "I love my son," this is certainly ON, or true for me.

Once you have your ON statement, make a circle with the thumb and middle finger of your non-dominant hand. Press the tips of these fingers firmly together and make a hook with the index finger of your other hand. Place the hooked finger of your dominant hand in the circle where the thumb and middle finger meet in your non dominant hand and pull. Hold the circle strongly and mentally state this to yourself, "Holding the circle strong means ON or that something is true for me." Then, say the opposite of this statement (for me, this would be "I don't love my son"), pull again and let your finger circle break. Now affirm that collapsing or letting your finger circle go means OFF or untruth to you. Lock the setting of both these ON and OFF symbols into your mind.

I simply tune into my general musculature and see if my muscles feel strong when I think about doing a certain activity. Sometimes I imagine holding my arms out to the sides and if they feel strong when I think about something, then I imagine that is a good thing for me. If my arms feel like they're going to sink down at the thought of something, or not hold strong, I interpret that as testing weak.

Whatever method you use, once you have the 'rules' for assessing the wisdom of your body, you can use this body wisdom to test for lots of different things – what to eat, whether to reply to someone on a dating site or whether to buy a certain book in the bookstore. Do this by making a statement: 'eating this sandwich' or 'going to this event' or 'dating this person' and then test your muscle strength.

If you have made a strong intention to be abundant, you can ask whether certain actions or thoughts are in resonance with that by saying, 'doing this activity will bring abundance' and see if your muscles support this.

LANGUAGE

Listening to your language will also give you clues as to your state of resonance. Changing your language can increase your ability to take responsibility for your life and become a more deliberate creator. Tune into yourself as you're talking today. Are you using words like 'have to' or 'should' or 'can't?' People who deliberately create use words that mirror that state of empowerment. Here are some turnarounds you might want to try out.

"I choose not to spend my time that way," versus "I don't have time."

"I choose to let my money accrue" versus "I'm too broke to buy that."

"I am choosing to do 'X' because it's Right for me" versus, "I have to do this."

Hopefully this chapter has given you a deeper understanding about how to use the tools I've described to everyday situations. Start using them in your own life and you will experience their power.

Chapter 8

STEPS, TOOLS AND RESOURCES

"Men are not distured by things, but the view they take of things."
—Epictetus

So far, I have described many steps, tools and techniques for creating abundance. I thought it might be helpful in this chapter to summarize them so you can have a quick reference for future use.

SUMMARY OF STEPS FOR CREATING WHAT YOU WANT

- Become intentional. Accept that you are creating your reality all the time and decide to become deliberate about the process.

  As I said earlier, accepting that we attract what we have by the energy of our vibrational field is the beginning place. Without a true understanding of this and a commitment to create differently, we will continue to feel like recipients or victims of what the world brings towards us.

- Open your heart to your own deservingness.

  Make sure your inner soil is fertile with deservingness. Otherwise, even if you are able to seed one of your dreams, its roots won't be able to burrow down into your soil and form a strong enough foundation to grow and thrive.

- Move into a lush state of gratitude.

Someone in a gratitude teleclass I was in once put it this way: "Abundance equals gratitude squared." I couldn't say it better.

• Clarify what you want to create as specifically as you can.

Although it's fine to imagine specifics such as the amount of money you'd like to make in a year, I always like to focus on the essence of what I'm imagining that specific is going to create: e.g., peace of mind, security etc. When I do that, I become aware of my deepest desires. Fulfilling one or two Soul desires is so much more satisfying than satisfying a dozen personality desires. As I say to clients, "It's hard to get enough of what we don't really want."

Check your desire for soul compatibility, then recalibrate your mental and energetic systems to ensure that every thought, action and feeling is in alignment with your desire.

Being in complete energetic alignment will bring what you want towards you effortlessly and easily.

• Give over the 'how' to your spiritual helpers.

We are so used to working our lives from our heads that it's difficult for us to not use our minds to figure out how we're going to make a dream come true. Focussing on the how is dangerous. It is dangerous first of all because even though our minds can create wondrous things, the universe is far more powerful and creative. Also, sometimes our minds, because of their limited perspective, may try and tell us why certain dreams can't happen and convince us to give them up.

Once we've formulated our dreams, we need to hand them over to the universe. The process is similar to being in a restaurant. Once you order your meal, you don't fret about how the cook is going to make it or whether it's going to come, you simply wait happily for the food to arrive on a plate. It's the same with our dreams. Make them, then release them to the vast creative power of the universe and/or your Spiritual Helpers.

Analise Rigan, who was a member at Findhorn for many years tells a story of a time she was wanting to express her creative self. "I didn't have a clue how this could happen," she said, "after all, I was a single parent and had to bring in money for us to live. I was a painter but I couldn't see how I was going to make money from that. So I asked God to show me in a clear way. The very next morning, a man I had never met phoned me. He had seen a picture I had done and been so affected by it that he'd called. When he asked me what my dream for my work was, I told him it was to get back to my creativity. He offered to financially support me for a little while. I could hardly believe my ears."

Analise says that even though getting the financial support was wonderful, the most important part of the experience was the feeling that God had answered her. Yes, God does do delivery.

Whatever names you apply to your Spiritual Helpers, whether it be angels, guides, Spirit, your Truth, the Source – all the spiritual support you could ever need is waiting for you. The names don't matter. In fact, sometimes, the names can get in the way. For example, in the early days of my spiritual development, when I heard people talk about their 'Guides', I found myself rolling my eyes. I just didn't like the term. I could, however, accept the idea of a Spiritual Presence. That concept resonated with me better. I had experienced the feeling of an omnipotent Spiritual Presence a few times, so the term worked for me.

As I moved along my spiritual path, other terms began to work also and now, I have come to accept all kinds of spiritual 'guidance' and am often aware of the variety of spiritual energies running through my world and the world around me. Not only am I now able to access these energies, but I also work with them on a daily basis. Knowing that I am not alone has had huge meaning for me.

If believing in Spiritual helpers is new to you, let me say this: all that's important is that you be open to believing. If you are open, your spiritual helpers will come to you. Your openness will be the invitation they need to enter your life and world. And when they do, you will know by the way things will start to flow. And you will know by the way bliss will begin to blossom in your heart.

As I mentioned earlier in the book, developing a relationship with your Spiritual Helpers may require time and/or a shift in consciousness. Learning to listen to how they speak to you may require a whole new set of listening skills. If you have been closed off to this side of yourself, the communication lines may be down and the access may be difficult. The spiritual side of you may have had to resort to speaking vicariously, through your friends, or through physical symptoms, or through internal nudges like the one that may have prompted you to buy this book. It will be helpful if you can drop your ideas of how your Spiritual Helpers should talk to you and simply open your heart to how they already are talking to you. The rest will unfold.

OTHER GARDENS

There are many web sites that offer phenomenal growth experiences. Seeing what other master gardeners have done with their inner soil is not only inspiring, it can give you ideas about how to create bigger blossoms in your own. Although I could have listed hundreds of web sites, here are the ones that were most meaningful to me in writing this book.

Abraham
www.abraham-hicks.com
Abraham, channeled by Gerry and Ester Hicks, has been an important resource for people wanting to create their own reality. Their site is complex with many offerings.

Byron Katie
www.thework.com
Byron Katie's web site offers both a description of her process, plus online worksheets and downloads. It also offers access to her books, as well as supportive chat groups.

David Cornfield
www.soulmaking.com
David is a psychotherapist and workshop leader who helps people reach their full potential.

David Spangler
lorian.bigmindcatalyst.com/
David Spangler, who has written extensively about the process of manifestation and creation, is part of The Lorian Association. Self-described as educators, The Lorians offer ideas and courses to renew and energize a co-creative relationship with the sacred. They offer courses to develop consciousness

which is "soul-infused and anchored in a spirit of individual freedom and the power of unobstructed love."

Donna Eden

www.innersource.net

This web site describes in detail some of Donna's work with Energy Medicine and provides opportunities to purchase her and her husband's books, tapes and videos. There is a comprehensive energy medicine question and answer page and some audio links with great audio interviews.

EFT

www.emofree.com

This is the web site of Gary Craig, the founder of the Emotional Freedom Technique. It's rich with articles, case histories and information about EFT and other meridian-based therapies. It's well worth a visit.

Elyse Hope Killoran

www.spiritualpartnering.com

One of the most comprehensive sites on prosperity, there are many giveaways on this site, an opportunity to take free tele-classes on prosperity as well as read Killoran's prosperity newsletter.

The Findhorn Foundation

www.findhorn.org

An extensive web site offering all kinds of information about the foundation, its programs and vision.

www.findhornpress.com

Over 120 books, audio cassettes and CD's on a variety of spiritual topics.

Dt. Francisco Rosero

www.adamantinesystem.com

In 2000, Francisco Rosero founded AHS, The Adamantine Health System, using his own metaphysical experience, research and the teachings of the Universal Energy and Love Healing method, which originated in Tibet. He offers in-person and online classes in this work.

Glenda Green

www.lovewithoutend.com

Glenda Green's work describes her conversation with Jesus and outlines his many revelations to her, which she includes in her book, *Love Without End–Jesus Speaks.*

Janet Amare

www.mysoulpurpose.net

Janet Amare offers seminars, coaching, healing and tools to support "healers" in every walk of life. She has much to offer around finding your life purpose.

LEAP-Life Energy Alignment Process

www.lifeenergyalignment.com

Julie Henderling and Dr John Parker are the founders of LEAP, the Life Energy Alignment Process. Their web site has valuable e-books, energy tools and downloads on VAT (Vibrational Alignment Technique) and EFT (Emotional Freedom Technique) plus information about their philosophy, trainings and courses.

Leslie Temple-Thurston

www.corelight.com

This site offers full-length chapters of Leslie Temple-Thurston's book and some descriptions of how to use the polarity and other techniques she describes.

Patricia Cota-Robles

www.1spirit.com

Patricia's web site has many articles, courses, free seminars and information on abundance and other spiritual topics.

Sanaya Roman

www.orindaben.com

Roman's site is very developed with lots to read and browse through. I particularly like the 3-4 minute meditations offered online, complete with music. There are also book excerpts, a Creating Your Highest Future Room and an Affirmations Room.

WRITTEN RESOURCES – BOOKS

The following books were all helpful to me in writing this one. Of course, these are only a few of the wonderful written resources that are out there.

Loving What Is, by Byron Katie

Manifesting With Your Angels, by Doreen Virtue

Do What You Love, the Money Will Follow, by Marsha Sinetar

You Were Born Rich, by Bob Proctor

Abundance Lives Inside of You, by Susan Smith Jones

Healing The Cause: A Path of Forgiveness, by Michael Dawson

The Findhorn Book of Forgiveness, by Michael Dawson

Energy Medicine, by Donna Eden

A Course in Life, by Joan Gattuso

The Abundance Book, by John Randolph-Price

Excuse Me, Your Life is Waiting, by Joan Grabhorn

Creating Money, by Sanaya Roman

Creating True Prosperity, by Shakti Gawain

Power versus Force, by David Hawkings

The Power of Now, by Eckhart Tolle

Everyday Miracles: The Inner Art of Manifestation, by David Spangler

Opening Doors Within, by Eileen Caddy

Chapter 9

MONEY AS FERTILIZER

"The time will come when you will satisfy a need for money by steadfastly
depending on the Master Self within – and not on anything in the world
of form. Until you do this, you will continue to experience
the uncertainties of supply."
— John Randolph Price in *The Abundance Book*

To me, money is stored energy. Each coin or bill is like a little battery cell
that can be used to make things happen in the world. Because money has
such energy, it is a power unto itself and, therefore, deserves a chapter in its
own right.

Sometimes I feel sorry for money. So much is being asked of it. People
expect it will make them feel successful, powerful and attractive. They demand
that it make up for all the areas in their lives that aren't working. And money
willingly tries to do all that. Sometimes it even succeeds for a while. As a
result, it is sometimes worshiped and chased after, but unfortunately, even if
money has come through and created some powerful feelings, it can't usually
sustain them. Not for long. Then people get mad at it. They blame it for being
the root of all evil and there's been many a pulpit that's cursed it even as the
collection plate was being passed around. And fights over it have caused many
a conflict and broken marriage.

Perhaps because of all these difficulties and complications, many spiritual people have chosen not to have a lot to do with money. They told themselves that money wasn't spiritual and minimized their need for it. Those who had money were apologetic about having it and sometimes felt as guilty about their bounty as nuns with vibrators.

By default, the acquisition and management of money has been left to people who are not necessarily on the spiritual path. With no evolved consciousness to guide its use, money has been used to do all kinds of things that are disharmonious and destructive. Thanks to the work of many people in the area of prosperity and abundance, this is changing. This is good news for when money is paired with consciousness, the results can only be life-affirming and positive.

Patricia Cota-Robles, author of many books on various aspects of spirituality and abundance, encourages people to rethink their relationship to money. A firm believer in the maxim 'what goes around comes around,' she suggests that if we want to have more money coming towards us, we give more money away. She also suggests that as we give money away, we visualize it coming back tenfold. So, if you give away a hundred dollars, imagine $1000 of it being returned.

One way of giving away money is to tithe. Tithing involves taking one-tenth of your income and giving it away. You can give it to a charity of your choice or you can give it to people you want to support, it really doesn't matter – the very act of doing it will move you to a place of greater trust in the universe and the laws that govern it.

Tithing, however, is just one way of loosening up rigid old habits that are keeping you from having a more abundant relationship with money. It's good to free up how we handle money because our behavior around money often conforms to rules that no longer serve us. Money has a lot of power in our culture, therefore a lot of rules have been developed around the use and flow of it. I invite you to flip the game board you've been playing on and try out some new behaviors. Here are some that will shake up your old habits and stimulate the flow of money in your direction:

- **Spend anyway**

Please know that as I suggest this, I am in no way supporting more consumerism. What I want to state here and state clearly, is that money needs to move. The more you put into the spinner, the more will come spinning back. In my own life, I know of no better way to get my financial life moving than to spend anyway. Spending anyway gives a huge note of confidence both to yourself and to the universe. It is a sure way of lighting up the neon sign on your forehead that says, 'Money recycling center. Bring your contributions here.'

On the other hand, if spending anyway increases your anxiety, the neon sign on your forehead may move from 'more money now' to 'I'm frightened about money' and that could obliterate your gains. So, if you are going to spend anyway, make sure you are still in your comfort zone – you may be right at the edge of it, but you need to be still in it. For many, this will mean spending without going into debt. Personally, I keep my debt to a minimum because I don't like the weight of debt in my life.

- **Spend money with a grateful heart.**

Don't begrudge spending the money you do spend, even if what you're spending money on is a bill that's owing. Be grateful that you have money to be sending out. Many people don't.

- **Keep a $100 bill in your pocket or purse.**

Seeing a large sum of money in your wallet or purse will help you to feel abundant. It's important to take your focus off the pennies, as the following story will illustrate. David Cornfield, an old friend, used to be a real penny pincher. He was a lawyer then with a 'license to steal' as one of his relatives used to say. Yet, despite this 'license,' he penny-pinched. Each time we went to an event, he'd take great care to half the cost exactly down the middle and then present me with my half.

David came from a poor family and had been taught frugality. To him, a penny saved was a penny earned. Since then, he's done a lot of work to create the life he wants and part of that involved letting go of his old attitudes to money.

"The problem with counting your pennies," says David, "is that it's the pennies you focus on. And what I focus on is what I get more of. I knew if I was going to create a more abundant life, I needed to let go of thinking about pennies and trust the flow of the universe. As it was, I was restricting that flow because of my fear."

Now David works as a psychotherapist and helps others to get in touch with the flow of the universe as well. He calls his business Creative Edge Counselling and his website is www.soulmaking.com.

• **Choose work and other activities from an energy of love, not from an energy of needing money**

One client I worked with hired me to help her make her business more financially successful. When we first talked, she complained that she was always just scraping by.

As we talked, it became clear to me that although this client wanted her customers to service her needs, she was only willing to do the bare minimum to service theirs. Of course, her customers sensed that and responded by being equally stingy, complaining about the amount she charged and often not paying her on time.

When my client shifted her focus to wholeheartedly contributing to her customers' well-being, they responded not only by rewarding her generously, but also by sending her other customers.

• **Always affirm your financial resourcefulness not your lack of it**

If you choose not to spend money on something, don't think, 'I can't afford this,' think 'I choose to let my fund accumulate,' instead.

• **If you get paid by clients, consider changing to a sliding scale of donation**

What I like about charging according to a sliding scale is that people are asked to do what's right for them. As a result, the money they do give comes from a place of offering, not obligation. I did this once and my income increased by 20%.

• **Tithe**

Giving away money is one of the surest ways of getting your financial situation moving. Tithing doesn't just have to involve money. You can also give away possessions, time, and the greatest gift of all, love.

• **Acknowledge the ways money facilitates your spiritual development**

Although spiritual searching always originates from an inner inclination, money can help us purchase the supports we need. For example, it was money that allowed me to sign up for my first yoga course and money that allowed me to go to Findhorn. Money is just energy and energy can be used to support spiritual and personal growth if you move it in that direction.

David Cornfield, says that when he first started his business, for example, he wouldn't take the time to market himself. "I had this self-righteous denial of needing money. But I soon realized that not having money was interfering with my life purpose. With it, I can evolve myself and help evolve others. That's what my life is about."

• **Acknowledge the ways money facilitates the world's spiritual development**

Money, when paired with spiritual consciousness, can change the world. I give regularly to environmental initiatives and the more money I make, the more I can give. If I won a million dollars, over half of it would go to causes of high consciousness. Imagine the power of that!

• **Skip the purchase**

Sometimes we buy something because we have an image of what that purchase will bring us: e.g., happiness, excitement, peace of mind. Play with the idea of creating the state without the purchase. Use the tools and techniques in the energy medicine chapter to simply create the state you want, without having to get it vicariously through the purchase of something.

• **Be a hearty receiver of the abundance that is already in your life**

There's a wonderful story in the Torah that describes a man who leads an exemplary, but frugal life. He takes pride in getting by with the bare minimum. When he gets to heaven, he's taken up on charges. Of course the man is furious and rants, "How can this be? I used so little!" "Exactly," his heavenly mentors cry. "God gave you so much and you hardly touched it. Do you think God would have offered you all that He did if you weren't meant to receive it?"

This story reminds me of times I've been with my son at a dinner party. He has a hearty and appreciative appetite and I can see how his enthusiastic love of the food always pleases the host who often presses more food on him, sometimes even giving him doggy bags to take home. His appreciation facilitates their abundance. A guest who only nibbled the food and hardly appreciated it would not have received this generosity. This is the same with all aspects of Life.

• Don't limit the universe

Let's say you want to manifest a new car: don't try to figure out how you're going to raise the money. First of all, it may be that you don't have to raise the money at all. It may be that you inherit a car when a relative dies or that you fall in love with someone who owns a car dealership. Leave the details to the other realms. All you need to do is be clear about your desire for the car, imagine it in your world, then give thanks for the fact that it's on its way.

Gary Craig, the founder of EFT, talks about this in the Palace of Possibilities on his web site: www.emofree.com. He says that trying to formulate the 'how' of making a desire come true is a major mistake. He argues that most people try to figure out how to achieve their goals before they begin conditioning their thoughts in the right direction. This is problematic because at this stage, people often can't find an acceptable 'how', and may well give up on affirming what they want. After all, who wants to affirm something that will only lead to a 'how' that is unacceptable?

In Craig's case, his 'how' would have included making more cold calls, getting up earlier in the morning, working on weekends, sacrificing time with his family AND calling on wealthier people that were "bigger than me. Oh my! How could I possibly call on business owners that had employees and were making more money in a month than I made in a year? Why would they listen to me?"

Gary Craig realized that if he had tried to figure out the 'how' ahead of time, he would have become discouraged and might have given up his dreams. Luckily for him, he spent no time thinking about the 'how' and put all his energy on realigning his thoughts. Then he let his inner wisdom take over and make it happen. He knew the 'how' would unfold quite naturally once the rest of him was in the right energetic state. As indeed it did.

• Remember the true Source of Supply

We need to be continually aware of the difference between the delivery system and the source of supply. Here's a story that will illustrate the difference. A few years ago, I had a thriving massage therapy business, but I felt as if the time had come for me to move on to other things. Because I imagined the massage work was the source of my income, I didn't feel free to give it up. It wasn't until I shifted into the realization that the massage work was merely the delivery system of the Source's abundance – not the Source itself – that I was able to give up the work. As soon as I did give it up, money flowed through other channels.

Many people mix up the delivery system from the Source when it comes to other things too – such as love. We do this by imagining that a specific person is the Source instead of just the delivery system of the Source. This can make it difficult for us to let go of people (and sometimes places) that aren't right for us and move on to the people and places that are right for us.

This is what happened to me when I lived at Findhorn. I had formed such deep and loving relationships there, I worried about all the love I was going to lose if I went back home. When I did move back to Canada, I realized that the friendships I made at Findhorn were simply the delivery system of a much bigger Source of love. These friendships were simply channels for that love and other channels would exist in other places.

Some people make the same mistake with money, imagining that it's the source of their financial well-being. I know from working with clients just how erroneous this is. I've had very wealthy clients and very poor clients and had them both resonating with the same amount of fear – the person with money was frightened of losing it and the person without was frightened of never having it. In my experience, it's the people who let it move through their hands, always trusting that there will be enough, who are the truly abundant ones. They are abundant because they know that money is never the source of financial security, it is only the channel.

- **Play the Prosperity Game**

This game, which you can play via the Internet, will weed out limiting beliefs you may have about money. There are several sites that offer it to people in a variety of different capacities. To explore more, just type "the prosperity game" into your search engine.

- **Lastly, but perhaps most importantly, Be the Love you Are**

Rachel Strauss, a good friend of mine, is a master of manifestation. "First of all, I get very clear about what I want," she says. "Then I give thanks for it. Giving thanks is crucial because gratitude and love are the same energy. And the most basic particles of the universe, the adamantine particles, respond to love. People need to understand that this is how the universe works. It's just like throwing an object in the air – you know it must fall. It's not happenstance – it's universal law. There are similar laws guiding how things come to us. When we act out of love, we are in tune with the basic particles of the universe. Those particles respond to love. They are love. Just as we are love. When we truly know that and come from that place, we can make anything happen. Even miracles."

The word 'adamantine' has been around for thousands of years. In the ancient Buddhist tradition, the word Vajrasattva means 'the Adamantine Being,' or the one who represents the Buddha of purification and healing. The dictionary defines 'adamantine' as something extremely hard and unyielding.

Those who have studied adamantine particles describe them as the fundamental building blocks of physical existence. Although scientists have yet to identify them (they are yet to be seen by even the most powerful microscope), proponents of their existence believe that adamantine particles comprise all that exists in our physical reality.

Glenda Green, who wrote *Love Without End – Jesus Speaks*, discusses adamantine particles extensively. She says that what makes them special is the fact that they are commanded by love. Therefore, when someone vibrates with the energy of love, their heart magnetizes adamantine particles. This is important in terms of abundance because adamantine particles are said to contain stored potential for the manifestation of any original substance or element, therefore, the more of them we have to play with, the more easily we will be able to create what we want.

So, when we vibrate with love, we fill our energy field with the fundamental building blocks of creation. Glenda Green suggests that we think of the heart as a magnet and love as the pencil. She says that when we are being Love, we can write our own destiny. And we don't have to work at making it happen either. When we are love, all things come to us through the power of magnetic attraction.

Adamantine particles are all around us, but we need a full heart and a willingness to interact more freely with life energies to attract them. When the Sacred Heart is activated, adamantine particles are magnetized and energy then floods the system. That's the reason that people who love what they do have such abundant energy!

The great teaching of the adamantine particles is to remember to do everything with love. At Findhorn, people often did a ritual before eating to bless the food. According to Peter Caddy, this blessing was more important than the type of food you ate. Healthy and vibrant to the end of his life, Peter ate a variety of foods and was sometimes disparaging of diets involving regimens like the macrobiotic diet because to his way of thinking, it didn't matter what you ate, as long as you ate it with love.

Glenda Green argues that it is the love we surround food with that "tells" the food how to nourish our bodies. In her belief, loveless meals cannot nourish. When love is present, however, it sets the body at a higher frequency, which facilitates the body not only in utilizing vitamins and minerals more efficiently, but catalyzes the body to manufacture them as well.

No wonder it is said that Love is the ultimate power in the universe.

Chapter 10

BECOMING ABUNDANCE ITSELF

"Forget your old ideas.
Forget the lies they told you.
Forget them all and you will begin to remember."
—Marianne Williamson

For most of this book I've been talking about how to create abundance. Now I want to go beyond that to an exploration of how to become abundance itself. This is where you get to when you move past conscious creating to the place of utter at-one-ment with abundance. You simply become abundance.

When I interviewed Tony Mitton, who lived in the Findhorn community for many years, he told me that although he'd been working with the laws of manifestation for years, and had become a very competent creator, he felt himself beginning to move beyond the act of creating abundance.

"At one point, I felt I was moving into a whole new state of consciousness where I began to act from a deep sense of attunement with Spirit," he said. "I began to do things in my life not from a desire to create my goals, but from a deep feeling of attunement to God." He gives an example. After he'd moved to Florida, he got 'guidance' to go to massage school. This was something he'd never considered before. It came to him in an intuitive way and because the impulse felt so right, he followed it. "As it turned out," Tony said, "being a massage therapist became a real fountain of abundance for me and the family, financially and in every other way."

To my mind, what Tony is describing is a willingness to surrender to a deeper knowing, a kind of Soul knowing. This Soul knowing may sometimes present us with ideas or situations that will expand us beyond our current ideas of ourselves. Although it's great to have the tools and techniques to self-direct and create the lives we want, if we don't open ourselves up to this greater knowing, we may be missing important opportunities or accepting lives less wonderful than our Souls might create.

When Tony went to massage school, he switched from directing his life from his personal ideas of himself, to having it directed from a place of attunement with his Spiritual Self. Some people might call this surrender. For me, the concept of surrender is relevant when we have been working our lives from a strong sense of ego. When the ego is used to running the show, the idea of working in alignment with our Spirit will certainly feel like surrender. But for those who haven't been using so much control, the merging with this deeper knowing may feel similar to the kind of relief you feel when you finally arrive home.

Sometimes, as with Tony, following the recommendation of our Spiritual Knowing is not difficult. This is not always the case. Sometimes following our deep inner truth can lead us to attract circumstances that test us to the depth of our emotional limits.

What happened to Steve Kauffman is an example. He was in the process of putting in a Watsu pool (for water shiatsu) when a deer fell into his pool. The liner was seriously damaged, and the subsequent repair was not only time-consuming, but expensive.

"I reacted with resistance," said Steve. "All I could think of was, 'Oh, shit! Why did this have to happen? Then, of course, more started to go wrong. This was not my picture of how it was supposed to be."

As the events unfolded, Steve found himself resisting and then letting go of his resistance, resisting, then letting go some more. Finally he dropped into a very deep place of letting go. "I began to have a much deeper appreciation for the entire process of letting go," he said. "Which is interesting, because that's what my work is all about. Now, in looking back, it was as if I was getting a huge lesson from my Soul."

He says that since then, he has been truly grateful for that. "Now I am more able to allow things to be as they are. I'm not as apt to try and fix and change and manipulate things, which goes against everything I've been taught. What I've been taught is to make things happen, to get what I want. The experience with everything not working got me into a far more fluid and allowing place where I could surrender and flow. When I talk to clients now about letting go and surrendering, it's coming from a much deeper place than before."

Eileen Caddy, the founder of Findhorn, had her own deep experience with letting go when she met Peter. She was meditating in a church one day when she heard a 'still small voice' speak to her from within. She knew if she followed that voice, drastic, emotionally difficult events would ensue, as indeed they did. Within a few months, she'd left her husband and four children and was writing down guidance to start a Center of Light that within a few short years, would become a Spiritual Mecca that affected thousands of people's lives, including mine. At this time in history, New Age concepts were not being touted from mainstream tv shows such as *Oprah* as they are now. Fifty years ago, getting guidance, even sitting down to meditate was considered strange. It must have taken incredible courage for Eileen to follow her inner voice.

Peter Caddy, on the other hand, had a firm belief in his intuitive nudges and was totally committed to following all of Eileen's daily guidance. He prided himself on his willingness to act in the moment and delighted in regaling people with his extraordinary manifestation stories. If he hadn't been so ready and willing to listen, and perhaps more importantly, to act on the guidance that Eileen was given, Findhorn would not exist.

"Leap and the net will appear," says Julia Cameron in her awesome book, *The Artist's Way*. The kind of leaping Julia is talking about, I believe, is not the risk-taking our ego sometimes pushes us to take, but Inspired Leaping. Inspired Leaping comes from our Soul which caws at us like some encouraging mother bird, prompting our fledgling Spiritual Selves to step off the branch of our current lives and fly!

Depending on the level of our Spiritual Attunement, inspired leaping can feel risky. Solid ground may disappear for a while. But just as the only way a bird can know the trustworthiness of the air is by leaping into it, we humans can only experience the trustworthiness of our spiritual path by jumping off the branch of what we know.

The Findhorn story has been inspiring to many. Janet Amare, a coach and Spiritual teacher, has never been to Findhorn, but told me in an interview that when she read about Peter and Eileen, she was deeply moved. "The Caddys' willingness to connect with Spirit and to move with what was being asked of them was profound and affected my own ability to follow my Soul. They introduced me to the idea that your Spirit is listening to you every moment of every day and that you can ask that Spirit for guidance in small things as well as the big things."

Eileen's willingness to tune into her Higher Knowing to guide her in every aspect of living intrigued me as well.

Here's my story. When I first heard of Findhorn, I was living in Toronto and was in a social service job that involved working with poor people. I was continually stressed and thought I'd try massage therapy to relieve some tension. Co-incidentally, the massage therapist I went to had just returned frm Findhorn and was full of enthusiasm for the place. As he talked, I had a strange knowing that I would be going there. And, sure enough, events in my life created an opportunity that spring to do just that.

When I arrived, I felt an immediate and pervasive feeling of being Home. I felt as if I was opening to an entirely new way of being. Although the experience was strong and part of me wanted to live there, I had just begun to develop my life as a writer in Canada, so I discounted the possibility of staying and returned home.

For months afterwards, I was plagued with dreams of deep grief over leaving Findhorn. But hey, I knew what my life was about, thank you very much, so I simply got on with creating it. A few years later, I was going to India to do a series of articles and, since the plane stopped over in London, I made a trip up to Findhorn for a quick visit. As soon as I arrived, the feeling of belonging instantly re-occured, but I had pictures to take and people to interview, so I ignored the feeling of kinship that was calling and went on my way.

Two days later, I was in Goa, India, with a friend who'd been in India for a few months. Since he knew his way around, and I was frightened of traveling alone in India, we decided to travel together. One night, I took one of Eileen's books on listening to your own inner voice to dinner with me. My friend wasn't interested in the book, and shared that he wanted to stay in Goa and sample more of the hallucinogenic enjoyments.

I wasn't at all interested in drugs and I was wondering what I was going to do, when I returned to my room and discovered it empty. Absolutely everything I owned – my camera, tape recorder, article notes, clothes, backpack, everything – had been stolen.

My only remaining possession, besides my money belt that held my passport, was Eileen Caddy's book. That felt like no small coincidence. Not knowing what else to do, I did what Eileen wrote about in her book: I went into meditation and asked for direction. I had never meditated to get guidance before, so this was new to me. When I asked what I should do, I was surprised when a clear message came, "Leave the person you're traveling with and go to Auroville."

Auroville is a spiritual community on the east side of India and since I'd heard Findhorn and Auroville were sister communities, I thought this idea made sense, but I was afraid. Going to Auroville would mean going back to Bombay. The idea of doing that alone was terrifying. When I'd landed there, I'd seem limbless beggars crawling along the sidewalk, people with open sores had pressed up against me and women had pushed deformed babies into my arms. It had been utterly overwhelming even with my seasoned companion there to guide me through it. How could I possibly go there alone? I was still in shock from the robbery and exhausted from jet-lag. I thought about simply flying home.

Thinking the guidance might have been incorrect, I went back into meditation. I voiced my fears and listened again. The voice was there again, as clear as ever, telling me that all would be well if I just went to the airport.

That seemed reasonable, so I plucked up my courage, said goodbye to my friend at dawn the next day and caught a boat to Bombay. Once I arrived, I went to a travel agent to book the flight.

"All the fights to Madras are sold out," the travel agent informed me.

What? I looked at him incredulously. Obviously this guidance stuff might work for someone as evolved as Eileen, but it didn't work for me. What was I going to do now? I felt a small, irate surge to rush back into meditation brandishing this new information with the indignation of a kid holding a non-functioning magic wand.

But where could I meditate? People were everywhere. Then I remembered what Eileen had done when she didn't have a quiet, private place and found a washroom. Most washrooms in India do not have toilets, but luckily for me, this one not only had a toilet, it also had a toilet stall, so I went inside, locked the door, put the seat down, and began to meditate.

I was agitated, but the voice was calm.

"Go to the airport," it said. "I'll arrange to get you on a flight."

Having no other clue about what to do, I followed orders. When I got to the airport by late afternoon, it was as busy as a department store on Christmas Eve. The lines were long and I had no idea which one to get into. Finally a lovely Indian woman saw my distress and offered to help. She disappeared into the crowd and when she returned, told me that there was only one more flight going to Madras that day, but that flight was full and had a 12 person waiting list.

"I got them to add your name, but you won't be chosen," she said, then moved her head in a kind of sideways figure eight. Many Indians seemed to do this with their heads. It was as if they are making the sign of infinity. She smiled and wandered back into the throng.

Gripped by anxiety, I found another washroom.

The 'voice' didn't seem the slightest bit perturbed. "All is well," it said. "All is very well."

"All is well? There's no flight! Now I'm going to have to find a cab back into town, find a place to sleep! I'm exhausted! Scared!"

"Stay here," the voice said. "You'll be on the flight."

And I was. How I was, I don't know, but I was.

I stayed in India another 2 months, listening to this guidance and following it along as I went. It was an entirely new way to live my life – so simple and graceful. And elegant.

Looking back, I can see how valuable the robbery was for me. I obviously needed to be stripped down to the bones of myself, to have my visible safety net disappear so I could feel the invisible safety net of spirit. It was an awesome lesson, one that I'm grateful for to this day. It opened me up to listening to myself and my Spiritual Knowing so much more deeply, which, in turn, led me to make another important decision a few weeks later: to go and live at Findhorn. I stayed in Findhorn for seven years, an experience which changed me for ever.

Now, when I think back on my Indian experience, I realize that the trip I got was vastly different from the one I had tried to create. Luckily, what I'd wanted to create hadn't hardened into a rigid set of expectations or, within that energetic, the robbery would have been a disaster. For me, however, the robbery transformed itself into a deep spiritual gift. And it certainly was a gift for someone else. It still makes me smile to think of some Indian enjoying my camera and tape recorder! The cost of replacing them was paltry compared to the invaluable gift of the spiritual lesson.

Many of the people I interviewed talked about how their own spiritual awakening had been catalyzed by the experience of not getting what they wanted. David Cornfield says that as he moves along his spiritual path, "it's less and less about getting what I want and more and more about knowing what I'm supposed to do. The problem about forming an intention is that it usually pulls me out of the present and has me looking to the future and how I want to shape it, but I don't want to do that anymore. I don't want to spend time imagining the future. What I want to do is get myself completely into the present tense and listen and respond to the music as it's playing right now."

Serene Chazan, a psychotherapist in California, puts it this way, "When I first started using the laws of attraction, it was wonderful. I remember sitting in my empty office, imagining clients and what it would be like to have some. I bought a big appointment book and did affirmations. Working the laws helped me to transform all the limiting beliefs my family gave me about money. I ended up making enough money to buy my house, which was a risk in a way, because I bought it during the time when the stock market was in a real mess. But I followed my intuition, which turned out to be right because when I sold the house a few years ago, it sold for twice the amount I'd paid for it."

Serene says that since she's done more spiritual work, she still sometimes uses the laws of manifestation to create something, but, for the most part, she likes to accept whatever comes her way. She uses her relationship with Steve, her partner, to illustrate. "There have been periods of time," she says, "when the relationship has not been what I've wanted and sometimes I've imagined trying to 'manifest' it differently. A few times I've even thought about leaving and 'manifesting' someone new. Then I had a realization – that the 'problem' with Steve was full of valuable lessons. It was teaching me that what I had to learn was to be abundant with myself and to pull on the abundance of God, instead of always making demands of Steve. This was huge for me. I am beginning to trust that even when I am not getting what my ego thinks is what 'I want,' I am getting what I need to get from a Soul perspective. Because abundance isn't just the good stuff, it's the hard times and the disappointments too – it's the whole enchilada."

What Serene is pointing out is that what the Soul wants and what the ego wants can be significantly different. So, when she didn't get what she thought she wanted with Steve, she trusted that she was being asked to stretch and grow in new, spiritual ways. With this change in consciousness, she doesn't feel so compelled to change Steve, but can accept and celebrate the relationship just the way it is. And to trust the process.

Reviewing this conversation with Serene, the key sentiment to me is about trusting the process. Trusting the process is a trait of the spiritually evolved. Many of the people I interviewed for this book have this trust. Some spoke of the fact that it was easier to have this trust when they lived at Findhorn than it was in the 'real' world. Silvia Shanahan, an ex-Findhorn member commented on this when I interviewed her.

"What I notice 'out here' is how fearful people are," Silvia said. "At times it's hard not to get overwhelmed by the mass consciousness of fear. Sometimes I have to tune it out like you might tune out a bad station on the radio."

Silvia goes on to explain how she manages to keep in a state of abundance despite all the energy of lack and fear around her. "I work on my inner state by creating a deep sense of peace and acceptance right down to a cellular level. I do this through meditation. I don't use affirmations because for me they're just not deep enough. And at times, I think they've been counterproductive because if you say something that your inner being knows isn't true, it weakens you."

Discoveries in the field of Applied Kiniesiology have shown this to be true: saying affirmations when the statements don't feel true does seem to have a weakening affect on the body. Dozens of studies have shown that when people are asked to make statements that aren't true, their muscles test weak, whereas when these people were asked to make statements that were true, their muscles showed strength and held firmly despite the pressure being exerted upon them.

Given this wisdom, perhaps we only need to focus on doing what feels true to us one moment at a time. If we do that, truly focus on the truth of each moment, we will ensure that each step is the right one and that the outcome will take care of itself. Whereas when we focus on the outcome, even though that outcome may be wonderful in terms of what the ego wants or thinks it wants, such a focus may cause us to miss out on some process that will take us far closer to our spiritual self.

Abundance is just so much bigger than outcomes as the following story will illustrate.

"It's funny," said Julie Howard, a Reiki practitioner who lives on Salt Spring Island in Canada. "I know a lot of people equate abundance with having things, but some of the times I've felt most abundant have been when I've had nothing. So for me, abundance has nothing to do with money or acquisitions."

When I first knew Julie, she was working for the Board of Education in Ontario and dreaming about the ocean. After a great deal of wrangling with herself, she finally decided to follow her heart and move west. When she got there, she was touring around to see where she might like to live when she discovered Salt Spring.

"I felt so totally at home there, but I wanted to start doing my healing work and thought I needed to be in a big city for that, so I went back to Vancouver.

"Once I was back in the city, I kept yearning for Salt Spring and the ocean. I was down to my last $150, but I decided to trust my intuition and go back there. When I arrived, I called about a place to stay and the guy told me I could have it for that exact amount – $150.

"I arrived at his place at night and after I gave him the money, I realized I had no money for food. In the morning, I went outside wondering what I was going to do when I saw that I was surrounded by fruit trees. I picked my breakfast from plum and apple trees. It began to rain very lightly and I could feel it on my face like fairy dust. Everything was golden and glistening and totally magical. All my terror just dropped away and I knew then how truly connected I was to the Source. And that everything comes from Source. It was an exquisite knowing."

Julie said that after that morning, this magical feeling stayed with her for several weeks. Also, many other incredibly synchronistic events happened to make her know just how truly she was being taken care of.

Many of the people I interviewed for this book spoke of such experiences. Once they allowed themselves to move into a state of deep attunement with their Spiritual Knowing, they were able to move forward in a graceful and elegant way. There was no struggle.

This at-one-ment can be a profoundly altering experience. Extraordinary things can occur in the magic of this consciousness. People often describe the experience as a waking up. It IS a waking up. A waking up to Spirit.

Given all that I've just said, is there any reason to use the laws of attraction at all? Wouldn't one want to simply bypass the act of creating and just become the creation through inner attunement? Although the yearning for complete at-one-ment with Spirit will always be there, I remind myself that I did arrive here with a body and a personality and I still have to deal with living in the world. Being able to create what I need can come in very handy sometimes. So I am happy to use the laws of abundance to create what I know is Right for me but as much as possible I stay open to being created by the deep wisdom of my spiritual knowing.

Whether I am creating or being created, it really doesn't matter. I just like the feeling of being locked in the arms of my Spiritual self, dancing to the music of the universe. Sometimes that's a fast dance and we have to move quickly to keep up with each other and sometimes it's a slow dance and all we have to do is lean into one another and enjoy the sweet sounds. Sometimes my worldly self leads and sometimes my spiritual self leads. More often than not, we move as one.

In closing, that's my wish for you as well: that you become one with your deepest truth and Spiritual Knowing. Then, abudance will not be something you 'create' but will be just What You Are.

*Chakras

The word chakra is Sanskrit for wheel or disk and signifies one of seven basic energy centers in the body.

If we were able to see the chakras (as many psychics do) we would observe a wheel of energy continuously revolving or rotating. Some poeple perceive chakras as colorful wheels or even flowers with a hub in the center. The chakras begin at the base of the spine and finish at the top of the head. Fixed in the central spinal column they are located on both the front and back of the body, and work through it.

Each chakra vibrates or rotates at a different speed. The root or first chakra rotates at the slowest speed, the crown or seventh chakra at the top of the head at the highest speed. Each chakra is stimulated by its own and complimentary color, and a range of gemstones for specific uses. The chakra colors are of the rainbow; red, orange, yellow, green, blue, indigo and violet.

about KAREN hood-caddy

her other books

Tree Fever (ISBN 0-929141-53-9)
Flying Lessons (ISBN 0-929141-80-6)
The Wisdom of Water (ISBN 0-929141-09-1)

her work

Over the twenty-five years of her professional career, Karen has worked with people individually and in groups to empower them to reach their full potential.

Karen helps people listen to the truth of themselves and how to support them taking appropriate risks. She also helps people stay centered and motivated and make their dreams come true. She is particularly good at helping people unblock and reach creative goals.

When she is not coaching, she loves to write. Her articles and stories have appeared in Europe, USA and Canada. She is very good at helping people unblock and reach creative goals.

Karen has a BA in Psychology, is a certified Self-Empowerment coach as well as a Wellness & Lifestyle Consultant. She has studied a variety of health modalities in Scotland (Findhorn), Switzerland, France and the US. She has established and helped others establish a number of successful small businesses.

Karen is fun to work with, motivating and full of heart.

CONTACT KAREN

karen@personalbest.org
www.personalbest.org

For further information about the Findhorn Foundation
and the Findhorn Community, please contact:
Findhorn Foundation
The Visitors Centre
The Park, Findhorn IV36 3TZ, Scotland, UK
tel 01309 690311
enquiries@findhorn.org
www.findhorn.org

for a complete Findhorn Press catalogue, please contact:
Findhorn Press
305a The Park, Findhorn
Forres IV36 3TE
Scotland, UK
tel 01309 690582
fax 01309 690036
info@findhornpress.com
www.findhornpress.com